Twayne's United States Authors Series

Sylvia E. Bowman, *Editor*

INDIANA UNIVERSITY

Robert Penn Warren

TUSAS 69

ROBERT PENN WARREN

by CHARLES H. BOHNER
University of Delaware

TWAYNE PUBLISHERS
A DIVISION OF G. K. HALL & CO., BOSTON, MASS.

PS
3545
. A748
Z6
(3)

To
JEAN

Contents

Preface

IN HIS ESSAY on Coleridge's *The Ancient Mariner,* Robert Penn Warren turns aside for a moment from the main line of his argument to appeal to "the principle of presumptive coherence in development, the fact that, despite waverings and false starts, a writer's history usually shows us a basic line." This same principle of presumptive coherence supplies the basis of organization for the present study, for Warren has shown a remarkable consistency in his development as a writer. In the forty years since he published his first poem in *The Fugitive,* he has followed with integrity and singleness of purpose the bent of his genius.

Because Warren's writing does form, to an unusual degree, a highly unified body of work, I have taken up his writings as nearly as possible in the order that they appeared. This plan has not been without its difficulties, for Warren has made a significant contribution to fiction, poetry, criticism, biography, and drama. But despite the variety of his forms, his work has centered on several basic themes: the problem of evil, the meaning of history, the human penchant for violence, the search for self-knowledge, and the need for self-fulfillment. These themes he has returned to again and again, exploring them with a depth of perception and a richness of illustration which have placed him among the major literary figures of his time.

This study is quite frankly an introduction. It aims at providing an overview of Warren's literary career, an analysis of the themes which have preoccupied him, and an account of the development of his art as it has deepened and matured. I am aware that there are aspects of Warren's career that have not been treated in detail. For example, he has been during a large part of his life a teacher, or part-time teacher, of English, and his students with whom I have talked have uniformly praised his teaching. In connection with his work within the university, he has issued at intervals a number of extraordinarily influential textbooks. The best known of these, *Understanding Poetry* (1938), written in collaboration with Cleanth Brooks, revolutionized the teaching of poetry in the colleges and universities by recalling professors and students from peripheral concerns to the actual subject of their study—the poem itself.

But the nature and significance of Warren's contribution to pedagogy will have to wait for a more detailed study than the present one. Such a study will undoubtedly appear, for the amount of commentary on Warren's work is growing as the magnitude of his achievement becomes better known. In the course of writing this book I have profited from much of the criticism that has appeared, and I have tried to acknowledge my indebtedness in the notes and bibliography. I have found particularly helpful the work of Cleanth Brooks and Leonard Casper. Mr. Casper's book, *Robert Penn Warren: The Dark and Bloody Ground* (1960), is the first full-length study of Warren to appear, and I have especially depended on his excellent bibliography.

I wish to thank Bruce Dearing, Dean of the School of Arts and Science of the University of Delaware, for his interest in and encouragement of this study. I am grateful to the Faculty Research Committee of the University of Delaware for a grant which enabled me to undertake research during the summer of 1961. I should also like to thank the members of the staff of the Hugh Morris Library for efficient and generous assistance.

My greatest debt is to my wife, Jean Astolfi Bohner, who has encouraged and assisted me in every stage of the preparation of this study.

CHARLES H. BOHNER

University of Delaware
Newark
November 23, 1963

Acknowledgments

Grateful acknowledgment is made to the following for permission to use quotations:

Random House, Inc., for excerpts from Robert Penn Warren's *Night Rider, At Heaven's Gate,* "Introduction" to the Modern Library edition of *All the King's Men, World Enough and Time, Brother to Dragons, Band of Angels, Promises, Segregation, Selected Essays, The Cave, You, Emperors, and Others, Wilderness, The Legacy of the Civil War.*

Harcourt, Brace, and World, Inc., for excerpts from Robert Penn Warren's *All the King's Men* and *The Circus in the Attic.*

The William Morris Agency for excerpts from Robert Penn Warren's *Selected Poems, 1923-1943.*

Appleton-Century-Crofts, Inc., for excerpts from *Modern Poetry: British and American,* edited by Kimon Friar and John Malcolm Brinnin.

Harper and Row, Inc., for excerpts from *I'll Take My Stand,* edited by Louis D. Rubin, Jr.

Viking Press, Inc., for excerpts from *Writers at Work,* edited by Malcolm Cowley.

Louisiana State University Press for excerpts from Louise Cowan, *The Fugitive Group: A Literary History.*

Vanderbilt University Press for excerpts from *Fugitives' Reunion,* edited by Rob Roy Purdy.

Yale University Press for excerpts from Cleanth Brooks, *The Hidden God: Studies in Hemingway, Faulkner, Yeats, Eliot, and Warren.*

Chronology

1905   Robert Penn Warren, born in Guthrie, Kentucky, April 24; parents, Robert Franklin and Anna Ruth Penn Warren.

1921   Graduated from Clarksville, Tennessee, high school; enrolled at Vanderbilt University.

1923-   Active in Nashville "Fugitive Group."
1925

1925   Graduated from Vanderbilt University.

1925-   Graduate student at University of California (M.A., 1927).
1927

1927-   Graduate student at Yale University.
1928

1928-   Rhodes Scholar, Oxford (B. Litt., 1930).
1930

1929   *John Brown: The Making of a Martyr.*

1930   Assistant Professor of English, Southwestern College, Memphis; Married Emma Brescia.

1931-   Assistant Professor of English, Vanderbilt University.
1934

1934-   Assistant Professor of English, Louisiana State University,
1942   Baton Rouge; appointed Associate Professor, 1936.

1935   *Thirty-Six Poems*; founded with Charles W. Pipkin and Cleanth Brooks the *Southern Review.*

1939   *Night Rider*; Guggenheim Fellow (second fellowship awarded 1947-48).

1942   *Eleven Poems on the Same Theme*; Professor of English, University of Minnesota, Minneapolis.

1943   *At Heaven's Gate.*

1944   *Selected Poems, 1923-1943*; Chair of Poetry, Library of Congress.

1946 *All the King's Men* (Pulitzer Prize).

1950 *World Enough and Time;* Professor of Playwrighting, Yale University (resigned 1956).

1951 Divorced Emma Brescia Warren.

1952 Married Eleanor Clark.

1953 *Brother to Dragons: A Tale in Verse and Voices.*

1955 *Band of Angels.*

1957 *Promises: Poems 1954-1956* (Pulitzer Prize, National Book Award, Edna St. Vincent Millay Prize of American Poetry Society); *Segregation: The Inner Conflict in the South.*

1958 *Selected Essays.*

1959 *The Cave;* elected to the American Academy of Arts and Letters.

1960 *You, Emperors, and Others: Poems 1957-1960; All the King's Men* (drama).

1961 *Wilderness; The Legacy of the Civil War;* Professor of English, Yale University.

Robert Penn Warren

CHAPTER 1

Southern Man of Letters

NO OTHER American literary figure of the twentieth century has exhibited greater versatility than Robert Penn Warren. In commenting on Warren's place in the world of letters, a reviewer once called him the "pentathlon champion" of American literature, for he has made a distinguished contribution to fiction, poetry, drama, criticism, and biography. While arguments about his preeminence in any one field would be ultimately inconclusive, his total accomplishment in all five surpasses that of any other living writer. This versatility, however, has cost Warren some of the critical attention accorded his great contemporaries. The literary critics, with their penchant for categorizing writers by genre, have often referred to Warren as if he were a genial and talented interloper who had trespassed momentarily on their preserve but who was really committed to a genre other than the one they were discussing.

The literary historians also have found Warren a troublesome figure. The lines of demarcation in the literary history of this century have been the two world wars. The generation of distinguished novelists which appeared immediately after World War I—Hemingway, Fitzgerald, Faulkner, Dos Passos—were all born between 1896 and 1899, saw service during World War I, and wrote during the 1920's and 1930's the books on which their reputations largely rest. Their early fiction attests to the impact the war had on them. Hemingway's *A Farewell to Arms*, Faulkner's *Soldiers' Pay*, and Dos Passos' *Three Soldiers* all deal with young men and women wrenched from the familiar world of inherited values and mangled by the machine of modern war. Although Fitzgerald had not seen the fighting, his fiction evokes the same sense of futility and despair which pervades the novels of the war. Since World War II, critical attention has been focused on young writers who, like their famous elders, found their first subject matter in their war experience.

The career of Robert Penn Warren falls between these two generations. He published his first novel, *Night Rider*, in March, 1939, the same month that Hitler entered Prague—scarcely a propitious moment for a tale of the Kentucky tobacco country at the turn of the century. Warren's second novel, *At Heaven's Gate*, found few readers, despite a splendid critical reception when it appeared in 1943. In tone and temper it marks a return to the 1920's, to all the sad young men of Hemingway's *The Sun Also Rises* and of Fitzgerald's *The Great Gatsby*. Warren's novel shows the influence of these earlier works and, in my view, can stand comparison with them, but its futilitarian tone doomed it with the public in the heroic year of Tarawa and the invasion of Sicily. When *At Heaven's Gate* was followed the next winter by Warren's *Selected Poems, 1923-1943*, the appearance of the two works within a year would, in more settled times, have been a publishing event of a magnitude calculated to establish his reputation at a stroke. But it was not until the publication in 1946 of *All the King's Men*, a novel generally conceded to be a classic of our times, that he began to receive the recognition that was long overdue.

Warren's place in our literary history can most profitably be assessed by seeing him in the context of that remarkable phenomenon, the Southern Literary Renaissance. The South may feel it is retreating on many fronts, but one fact is indisputable: it has seized possession of the American literary scene. To demonstrate this proposition, it is only necessary to call the roll of Southern writers in this century. Among literally dozens that might be named, perhaps the most prominent are William Faulkner, Ellen Glasgow, Thomas Wolfe, Katherine Anne Porter, Eudora Welty, Conrad Aiken, Erskine Caldwell, Elizabeth Madox Roberts, Stark Young, James Branch Cabell, Richard Wright, John

Gould Fletcher, DuBose Heyward, Tennessee Williams, and Ralph Ellison. As soon as we add the name of Robert Penn Warren to the list, we are reminded of the group with which he is inevitably associated, the Nashville Fugitives, that loosely defined circle of writers teaching and studying at Vanderbilt University in the early 1920's which included, among others, John Crowe Ransom, Allen Tate, and Donald Davidson. No single region of the United States has been able to boast such a distinguished group of authors since the Concord-Cambridge circle of the middle of the last century.

Even if we should be inclined to doubt the worth and permanence of modern Southern writing, we should still have to account for the stubborn historical fact that so much has been written by Southerners and, in this age of criticism, that so much has been written about them. The South has also managed to carry off more than its share of literary prizes, led by Faulkner's Nobel Prize. Southerners have won eleven Pulitzer Prizes for fiction, five for poetry and four for drama. And Robert Penn Warren is the only writer to have received the Pulitzer Prize for both fiction and poetry.

The causes of the Southern Renaissance have been the subject of much debate and conjecture. There were, of course, literary stirrings in other parts of the country at much the same time. The early years of the century saw the emergence of a Midwestern or "Hoosier" school of fiction and poetry, and at the same time Chicago was rising to prominence as a center of literary activity. New England held fast to its already well-established place in American literary life, and New York City continued to assert its literary supremacy. But still, there has been something special about the South.

Young Southerners, first of all, have been determined to win for the writer the respect and dignity which the Old South denied him. Before the Civil War the career of man of letters in the South simply did not exist. As Thomas Nelson Page observed in *The Old South,* "where literature was indulged in it was a half apologetic way, as if it were not altogether compatible with the social dignity of the author."[1] Nowadays, however, there is discernible among Southern writers the union of a sense of vocation with a sense of mission.

But the roots of the Renaissance go deeper. The circumstances of Southern history, its cavalier myth and its violent and tragic destiny, provide an inexhaustible subject for the writer. The South alone among American regions has known military defeat and occupation. In a society which places great value on success and progress, only the South has known cataclysmic failure. Given such a situation, Southerners would naturally brood upon the tragic dimensions of life.

Ringed round by a culture toward which it feels alien and hostile, the South has drawn in upon itself, cultivating its uniqueness and deepening its sense of community. Although the region has produced a bewildering diversity of talented writers, they yet share one thing in common—a deep attachment to and a sense of place. The importance of the small town in Southern life, the pride in family and region, and the sense of a rich and gallant past have combined to give the texture of life in the South a special density and coherence. Southerners share a body of allusion, an inherited sense of order, and a unity of feeling which provides a tremendously valuable matrix for literature. Such a society, however, is not without its perils. For a closed society, like a clannish family, can exact demands and insist on allegiances which the fiercely independent artist may find intolerable. Thus the milieu in which the Southern writers function is at once nurturing and stultifying. Even in revolt from his region, the Southern writer has felt himself compulsively drawn to articulate its meaning. Thomas Wolfe rebelled furiously from the South; Ellen Glasgow rebelled and was reconciled. The tension generated by the opposing forces within Southern society is one of the central facts in the work of Robert Penn Warren.

I

There is not, of course, one South, but many: tidewater, uplands, cotton belt, delta, industrial center. The South of Robert Penn Warren is the hill country of Kentucky near the Tennessee border, a section known as the Black Patch because of the "dark fire-cured" tobacco grown there. It is a land of moderate-sized farms, varying from gently rolling fields, ripe green with tobacco, to scarps and rocky hillsides forested with cedar and sycamore. The land was settled by pioneers from the Southern uplands who crossed the Alleghenies toward the close of the eighteenth century and settled the Cumberland country.

It has not been sufficiently noted that Warren's work forms a history from the early nineteenth century to the present of the South he has known best. While it has neither the geographical nor the genealogical coherence of Faulkner's Yoknapatawpha or of Ellen Glasgow's Queensborough—and there is no indication that Warren ever intended to create an American Wessex—his work nevertheless forms a panorama of a usable past covering more than one hundred and fifty years of Southern history. As he once told an interviewer: "It never crossed my mind when I began writing fiction that I could write about anything except life in the South. It never crossed my mind that I knew about anything else; knew, that is, well enough to write about. Nothing else ever nagged you enough to stir the imagination."[2]

Warren fully shares the Southern feeling for family, the sense of the continuity of generations; for his own roots in Southern history and experience are deep. This interest appears in his fiction in the attention he devotes to the family trees of his characters. He is fascinated by the way a son may inherit his father's Roman nose, his quirks of speech, or his tendency toward abstraction or violence. Characteristically, one of his early poems is entitled "Genealogy"[3] and is concerned with his grandfather, Gabriel Telemachus Penn, a veteran of the Civil War.

> Grandfather Gabriel rode from town
> With Grandmother Martha in a white wedding gown.
> Wine-yellow was sunshine then on the corn,
> But swollen ran the river, the hills were brown,
> And wind in the east, when a son was born. . . .

Both of Warren's grandfathers fought with the Confederacy in the Civil War, and throughout his childhood he heard stories

of the war told by people who had witnessed it. He can remember his grandfather reminiscing about the Battle of Shiloh:
"One hundred and sixty men we took in the first morning, son.
Muster the next night, and it was sixteen answered."[4] A similar
scene is evoked, affectionately, in Warren's poem "Court-martial."

> Under the cedar tree,
> He would sit, all summer, with me:
> An old man and small grandson
> Withdrawn from the heat of the sun.
>
> Captain, cavalry, C.S.A.,
> An old man, now shrunken, gray,
> Pointed beard clipped the classic way,
> Tendons long gone crank and wry,
> And long shrunken the cavalryman's thigh
> Under the pale-washed blue jean . . .
> I see him now, as once seen.

II

Robert Penn Warren was born April 24, 1905, in the tobacco
market town of Guthrie, Kentucky. His boyhood winters were
spent in town attending the Guthrie school and his summers in
the country on his grandfather's farm in Trigg County. In the
fall of 1920, he entered the high school across the border in
Clarksville, Tennessee, graduating the following spring at the
age of sixteen.[5]

The years of Warren's boyhood were a time of economic
turmoil in the Black Patch, a one-crop farming district—the entire
community depended wholly on the market price of tobacco.
When international tobacco trusts arbitrarily fixed prices for all
classes and grades of tobacco, the local planters fought back by
organizing their own associations. Attempting to force mavericks
into their fold, they formed bands of "night riders" to burn
barns and scrape plant beds. The ensuing violence led to the
establishment of martial law in Kentucky, and one of Warren's
earliest memories concerns an encampment of state guards who
had been called into Guthrie to preserve order. The melodrama
of the night-rider stories was a staple of his boyhood and later

provided the inspiration for his first published fiction, the early novelette, "Prime Leaf," and his first novel, *Night Rider* (1939).

A good deal of Warren's early education in literature was forwarded by desultory reading at home. He had, by his own admission, no interest in writing during these years, only in reading. He shared the usual boyish admiration for "Horatius at the Bridge" and "How They Brought the Good News from Ghent to Aix." He read a "great mixture of stuff, whatever happened to come to hand—the usual nineteenth century novelists, the Boy Scout books, . . . Darwin, thrillers, detective stories."[6] He knew intimately the King James Bible, and he has since advised young writers to read their own Bible and mark it well.[7] Warren also began to cultivate what would become a continuing interest in history. He read Gibbon and Macaulay, volumes on every Southern shelf, and was particularly captivated by the "extraordinary romance" of American history, devouring the multi-volume works of Prescott and Parkman. But his great discovery was H. T. Buckle's *History of Civilization.*[8]

> I read Buckle and then I could explain everything. It gave me quite a hold over the other kids; they hadn't read Buckle. I had the answer to everything. Buckle was my Marx. That is, he gave you one answer to everything, and the same dead-sure certainty. After I had had my session with Buckle and the one-answer system at the age of thirteen, or whatever it was, I was somewhat inoculated against Marx and his one-answer system when he and the depression hit me and my work when I was about twenty-five. I am not being frivolous about Marx. But when I began to hear some of my friends talk about him in 1930, I thought, "Here we go again, boys." I had previously got hold of one key to the universe: Buckle. And somewhere along the way I had lost the notion that there was ever going to be just one key.

In the autumn of 1921, Warren entered Vanderbilt University in Nashville, Tennessee, intending to study science. It was one of the remarkable strokes of good fortune in his career, as well as one of the happy coincidences of American literary history, that at that moment in time a number of talented people who shared an interest in writing poetry had come together in Nashville. Calling themselves the "Fugitives," the members eventually evolved the most influential American literary movement of the twentieth century. All discussion of the Southern Renaissance and, for that matter, the intellectual history of the South since the Civil War, inevitably returns to them. Warren has called their influence upon him during his formative years "extremely important."[9] Their magazine, *The Fugitive*, provided an outlet for his first published work, and his own subsequent career as writer, critic, and teacher has been one of the major factors in the group's influence on American cultural life.[10]

John Crowe Ransom, a native of Pulaski, Tennessee, and an alumnus of Vanderbilt, was the intellectual leader of the Fugitives. In 1921 Ransom, at thirty-three, had already demonstrated the gifts which would later enable him to wield vast influence on the national literary scene. In 1919 he had published a volume of verse, *Poems About God*; and, during the years Warren was an undergraduate, Ransom was writing the poems which he would bring out in 1924 under the title *Chills and Fever*. Since he was a published poet, a former Rhodes scholar, and the teacher of several members of the group, Ransom naturally exerted great influence among the Fugitives. He taught Warren in freshman English and the following semester invited him to enroll in "English 9," a course in advanced composition.[11] Excited by his work under Ransom and bored by freshman chemistry, Warren discarded his plans for a scientific career and began to study literature in earnest.

During the first quarter of his sophomore year, Warren was placed in Donald Davidson's survey course in English literature. Davidson, like Ransom a native of middle Tennessee and a graduate of Vanderbilt, was another member of the Fugitives. "I first knew Robert Penn Warren," he recalled in 1958, "when he turned up in an English class I was teaching—a freckled, angular, gawky boy, yet a prodigy whom at birth the Muse had apparently vested with a complete literary equipment."[12] Davidson encouraged Warren to develop his talent for writing, excusing him from the required term papers for the course and allowing him to write imitations of Chaucer and Beowulf:

Warren spent the second and third quarters of his sophomore year studying with Walter Clyde Curry.[13] After taking a doctorate at Stanford University, Curry had joined the Vanderbilt faculty in 1915. Although his approach to literature was philosophical and historical and his major contribution was to be in Chaucer and Shakespeare scholarship, Curry was also meeting with the Fugitives and writing poetry. Recognizing Warren's gifts, Curry lent him books, criticized his writing, and encouraged his interest in the Elizabethans, particularly John Webster and John Ford.

Their dedication to scholarship, however, had not dulled the members of the Vanderbilt English faculty to contemporary writing. When *The Waste Land* appeared in 1922, for example, it was called to Warren's attention at once by Donald Davidson, who brought him the copy of *The Dial* in which the poem appeared. And Warren had the advantage of discussing the new poetry with the young and enthusiastic faculty members under whom he was studying. The university had, of course, its limitations. It was, as Warren said later, "a small and close provincial college." Yet the fact that the truly gifted members of the faculty were few made their impact all the greater. "The limitations," Warren said, "made a kind of personal focus on individuals and on ideas; I remember this quite distinctly, since some of these people represented the great world of ideas and the great world of geography, of wider horizons, in a very special way which is no longer true in educational institutions."[14]

Equally significant for Warren's personal literary development during these years was the friendship of another undergraduate and fellow Kentuckian, Allen Tate. Tate was twenty-one years old and entering upon his senior year in the fall of 1921, the year Warren came to Vanderbilt. That year Tate had eagerly accepted an invitation from Davidson to join the Fugitives, for he had fallen under the spell of both Davidson and Ransom. "At that early age," he said, they "meant just about everything." Tate brought to the group the boldness of youth, a taste for the *avant garde* in literature, and a total commitment to poetry. For Tate, Warren said, it was "poetry or death."[15]

Tate has written an amusing account of his first meeting with Warren.[16] During the spring of 1923, Tate, busily typing a poem in the bachelor quarters of Walter Clyde Curry, saw a young man wander into the room, "the most remarkable looking boy" he had ever seen:

> He was tall and thin, and when he walked across the room he made a sliding shuffle, as if his bones didn't belong to one another. He had a long quivering nose, large brown eyes, and a long chin—all topped by curly red hair. He spoke in a soft whisper, asking to see my poem; then he showed me one of his own—it was about Hell, and I remember this line:
>
> Where lightly bloom the purple lilies . . .
>
> He said he was sixteen years old and a sophomore. This remarkable young man was "Red," Robert Penn Warren, the most gifted person I have ever known.

Tate, impressed by Warren's early attempts at writing poetry, insisted that he show them to the editors of *The Fugitive* and of *The Double Dealer,* a little magazine which had begun publishing in New Orleans in 1920. As a result, Warren soon had the satisfaction of seeing his work appear in both magazines. Led through his interest in Baudelaire and the French Symbolists to a close acquaintance with the work of Ezra Pound and T. S. Eliot, Tate communicated his enthusiasm for these writers to Warren. Tate's considerable influence on the younger Warren led several of the Fugitives to consider him a follower. "I am content for the moment at least," Warren wrote Tate, "and you should be happy for a bright disciple."[17] For his part, Tate never doubted Warren's genius. Speaking of some verses Warren had written for the book page of the Nashville *Tennessean,* Tate wrote Davidson: "That boy's a wonder—has more sheer genius than any of us; watch him: his work from now on will have what none of us can achieve—power."[18]

Tate introduced Warren to another member of the Fugitives, Ridley Wills. Will's undergraduate career had been interrupted by army service in World War I, and he had returned to the campus glowing with the prestige of a first novel entitled *Hoax.*

He was, in Tate's opinion, "small, graceful, ebullient, and arrogant, and one of the wittiest and most amusing [of] companions." The three friends determined to room together in Wesley Hall, a dormitory for theological students, and no place, Tate said, "for the Heathen." This period in their lives, as described by Tate, was wildly exciting, a mixture of undergraduate prankishness and serious intellectual discussion:[19]

> In order to get into bed at night we had to shovel the books, trousers, shoes, hats and fruit jars onto the floor, and in the morning, to make walking-space, we heaped it all back upon the beds. We stuck pins into Red while he slept to make him wake up and tell us his dreams. Red had made some good black-and-white drawings in the Beardsley style. One day he applied art gum to the dingy plaster and when we came back we saw four murals, all scenes from *The Waste Land*. I remember particularly the rat creeping softly through the vegetation, and the typist putting a record on the gramophone.

Wills and Tate began taking Warren to Fugitive meetings while he was still a sophomore, although he was not made a member of the group until the spring of his junior year. The meetings, held informally at the home of one of the members, were a revelation to the shy and impressionable Warren. The group was in earnest about the significance of poetry as a serious undertaking. "I got the feeling," Warren recalled, "that poetry was a vital activity, that it related to ideas and to life."[20] From the first, the discussions put great emphasis on a rigorous and searching attention to the structure of poetry. The author would read his composition aloud, while the members of the group followed the text from typed copies which had been prepared for them. Perhaps the reading might be followed by comments of a general nature or by a murmur of compliments, but more likely it was greeted by a ruminative silence. The discussion that followed was, by custom and agreement, skeptical and frank. The poem was subjected to an exhaustive and probing analysis, and any weakness in rhyme, rhythm, or imagery was ruthlessly exposed. The merely facile or conventional exercise in verse was likely to be dismissed without much comment. This habit of formalistic, intensive criticism undoubtedly shaped the habits of composition of the group and carried over into their private conversations concerning their work.[21] John Crowe Ransom employed a similar technique in his advanced writing courses, stressing theories of prosody and scrutinizing in detail selected poems from English literature. And this method of close textual analysis, broadened and systematized, provided the method of Warren's *Understanding Poetry* (1938), written in collaboration with Cleanth Brooks, a work which profoundly altered the teaching of poetry in college classrooms.

For Warren, association with the Fugitives not only offered a stimulus and a discipline but also provided an outlet for publication. During his junior and senior years, he published twenty-four of his poems in *The Fugitive*. And in his last year at Vanderbilt, he was asked to assume some of the editorial responsibilities. While grateful for the opportunities that association with the group afforded, Warren seems not to have been entirely sympathetic with the Fugitives and their methods. In the spring of 1924 he wrote to Tate: "I value your criticism a good deal more than any other I receive, for you know the sort that comes out in a Fugitive meeting." Warren's own youthful intensity and dedication to the Muse evidently led him to feel that certain members of the group lacked seriousness. He voiced his dissatisfaction in a letter to Tate:[22]

> As I expected, my poem Romance Macaber was rather poorly received by the majority of the members. "Morbid, affected, unconvincing"—were among various criticisms applied. Hirsch[23] with customary pomp inquired if the thing was not extremely personal: "the expression of an extremely personal passion and emotion, etc." I was compelled to reply that had it been I would never have read it to the company there assembled.

In 1956 Warren, in looking back on the Fugitive years, was amazed that the fellowship should have seemed to others a unified movement. "A few years after I left Vanderbilt, people began to refer to those people [the Fugitives] as a unit, as if there were a church or an orthodoxy. I was so shocked by that . . . because I was so aware of the differences of temperament, and the differences of opinions . . . but the notion of a unity had just never occurred to me, except that the unity was just purely a unity of friendship and common background."[24]

III

Upon graduating *summa cum laude* from Vanderbilt in 1925, Robert Penn Warren entered the University of California to undertake graduate study in English. If he had found cause for discontent with the Fugitives during his last year at Vanderbilt, it was soon dissipated in the atmosphere of Berkeley. He thought the literary men there "fifty years behind the times." At Nashville the talk had been all Pound and Eliot, but at Berkeley the campus intellectuals discoursed interminably about Marx and Engels.[25] Warren nevertheless settled into the routine of graduate work and in 1927 received his Master of Arts degree. He was now firmly committed to advanced study in English literature, and in the fall of 1927 he entered Yale for additional work.

During the summer of 1928, Warren was in New York visiting Allen Tate who, with his wife Caroline Gordon, was moving in the literary circle which included Scott Fitzgerald, Hart Crane, Edmund Wilson, and John Peale Bishop. Attempting to establish himself by free-lance writing, Tate had brought out a biography of Stonewall Jackson in the late spring of 1928 and was hard at work on a life of Jefferson Davis which appeared in November, 1929. Through Tate's acquaintanceship with the literary agent Mavis McIntosh, Warren secured a commission from the recently established firm of Payson and Clarke to write a biography of John Brown.[26] Warren plunged into the task with enthusiasm, and even made the trip to Harper's Ferry to interview the last surviving witness of John Brown's raid. *John Brown: The Making of a Martyr*, published in November, 1929, received a handful of good reviews, but it sold few copies in that disastrous season of the Great Crash.

Warren's life of John Brown is a substantial achievement and would have enhanced the reputation of a seasoned biographer. Considered as the first book of a young man of twenty-four and as one written while he was simultaneously engaged in graduate study, it is an astonishing demonstration of his precocity and his creative energy. The biography reveals how early Warren's special gifts matured: his ability to render a scene palpably and memorably, his insight into character, and his skill at wringing from a story every ounce of color and drama. Earlier biographies of Brown had tended to be written by either the prosecuting attorney or the counsel for the defense. Although Warren is clearly not in sympathy with his protagonist, he is obviously trying to be scrupulously fair in his weighing of evidence. Such weaknesses as the book possesses are those of the neophyte scholar. Warren has a tendency to lose sight of his hero in his zeal to untangle the skein of political history. He occasionally succumbs to the temptation to linger over a disputed point in the evidence at the cost of the movement of his narrative. And his balanced handling of his materials is sometimes marred by an obtrusive tone of youthful flippancy and heavy irony.

As Warren interprets Brown's career, he is a man laboring under a "profound compulsion," possessed by an idea and enamored of violence. Like his Puritan forebears, John Brown fancies himself one of the elect; and like those rarified descendants of the Puritans, the Transcendentalists, he surrenders himself to an idea without regard for its practical consequences in an imperfect world. Brown, in Warren's view, is a man blissfully untroubled by self-knowledge. In his stiff-necked insistence on being in the right, he represents a type which has fascinated Warren ever since: the man who possesses or develops an "elaborate psychological mechanism for justification" (446). Brown finds his justification in a single abstraction—freedom. "The word 'Freedom' obscured every selfish motive, and transformed . . . every act of criminality or violence into something worthy and excellent" (264). Sustained by his egotism, Brown was guilty of a "fundamental error." He "thought of slavery in terms of abstract morality, and never in the more human terms of its practical workings" (331). Other giants of the era, in Warren's opinion, were seduced by the same tendency toward abstraction: the young Lincoln, for example, "the shambling awkward Cassandra of Illinois," and Ralph Waldo Emerson, "a man who lived in words, big words, and not in facts." Finally, John Brown, donning the mantle of an Old Testament prophet, is a man who confounds means with ends.

> [John Brown's] own will and God's will were one. Hypocrisy is too easy a word to use here, and too simple. If John Brown had no scruple at deception it was because the end justified the means. That end, that goal, which beckoned year after year, seemed to float and shift and change its shape like some mirage. In other words, John Brown's enormous egotism expressed itself in one set of terms after another, and after Harper's Ferry there would be a final transposition of this egotism into new terms. In his past history these terms had become larger, more impersonal, more dignified, and justification under them had become easier. . . . Does man's will need justification beyond the will of God? (351)

John Brown is a contribution to American history, valuable and instructive in its own right. But for the student of Warren's career, it is chiefly interesting in the way it presages the characteristic preoccupations of his later work. The biography was, as Warren said later, a "step toward fiction."[27] The John Brown who emerges from Warren's pages is the spiritual ancestor of a number of the heroes of Warren's novels, and the biography adumbrates a number of the themes that he has returned to again and again. The man who single-mindedly follows an idea to a violent end, the man doomed by his lack of self-knowledge, the man caught in the dilemma of reconciling evil means with a desirable end—these form the thematic matrix of Warren's fiction.

IV

In the autumn of 1928 Robert Penn Warren sailed for England to take up his appointment at Oxford as Rhodes scholar from Kentucky. Warren had accepted the award with the knowledge that he was following in the footsteps of his teacher and fellow Fugitive at Vanderbilt, John Crowe Ransom, who had been at Christ Church College from 1910 to 1913. Another Fugitive, William Y. Elliott, later professor of government at Harvard, had been at Balliol College from 1921 to 1923. Elliott had served for a year as an English instructor at Vanderbilt and, together with Allen Tate, had introduced Warren to some of the new poetry.[28] Warren was joined at Oxford by another Vanderbilt alumnus and Rhodes scholar, Cleanth Brooks—the two friends there laying the groundwork for their long, distinguished collaboration.

It was an exciting time to be living abroad, but the experience brought Warren a sense of detachment concerning his life in Kentucky and Tennessee and a sense of nostalgia as well—"the look back home from a long distance."[29] In the spring of 1930 Warren received a letter from Paul Rosenfeld, who, with Van Wyck Brooks and Lewis Mumford, was editing the *American Caravan,* inviting him to submit a long story. Rosenfeld had heard Warren reminiscing about his boyhood memories of the night riders in Kentucky and had suggested that the stories would make excellent material for fiction.[30] As a result, Warren stole time from his academic work at Oxford to write "Prime Leaf," a novelette which Rosenfeld accepted and which appeared in the *American Caravan* for 1931.

"Prime Leaf" deals with the impact on a small boy of a quarrel between his grandfather and father over the terroristic tactics of an association of tobacco growers who have organized a band of "night riders" to resist a monopoly of Eastern buyers. The father's involvement in the scheme leads him to shoot one of the night riders and, ultimately, to be ambushed and murdered himself. The story is a polished performance which abounds with intensely realized scenes of the tobacco farms and small towns of Warren's youth. The narrative power which he had already displayed in his biography of John Brown is enhanced in the story by a talent for dialogue, a keen ear for the nuances of dialect and the rhythms of human speech. The reader finds, in embryo, themes that would continue to concern Warren: the ways of violence, the adaptation of means to ends, and the mixture of love, jealousy, and guilt in the relation of father and son. But Warren had not by any means exhausted the reservoirs of memory, for a decade later the themes only dimly shadowed forth in "Prime Leaf" were developed on a larger scale in his first novel, *Night Rider*.

During his temporary expatriation in England, Warren did not lose touch with the Fugitives in Nashville. Although their magazine expired in December, 1925, the leading spirits of the group, Ransom and Davidson, were teaching at Vanderbilt; and Tate, although living in New York, kept in close touch through correspondence. Louise Cowan, in her excellent study of the Fugitives, has shown that in the late 1920's they were becoming concerned over the course the South was charting in public affairs. During the early years of the decade, their interests had centered on poetry and philosophy, and in so far as they were conscious of being Southerners, they were intent on repudiating the magnolia-and-julep tradition of Southern letters. As the forward to the first issue of *The Fugitive* put it: "*The Fugitive* flees from nothing faster than from the high-caste Brahmin of the Old South." The contributors to the magazine would have condemned sectional identity as a provincial hindrance to their own development as artists and as men.

But as industrialism made greater inroads into the South after World War I, some of the Fugitives were growing increasingly dissatisfied with the direction the region was taking. In 1925 the notorious Scopes "Monkey Trial" in Dayton, Tennessee, had fostered the image of a bigoted and anti-intellectual South. Attacks in the Northern press, of which H. L. Mencken's "The Sahara of the Bozart" is the most famous, were baiting the South and its traditional ways. The Fugitives were distressed by what they considered to be the results of a culture based on the machine: the accelerating tempo of life, the chaotic individualism, the blatant materialism, the debasement of human effort and human dignity. The artist in such a society was particularly vulnerable, for the pressures of mass culture were corrupting taste and commercializing art.

It was just at this point that the history of the South offered a parable applicable to modern America. The South, even in defeat, had resisted the siren song of the machine and had clung doggedly to its agricultural ways. If, when judged against the

Yankee Cult of Success, Southern society seemed slow and backward, it nevertheless cherished the values of family tradition and grace of manner and nurtured the esthetic and spiritual impulse. The so-called "New South," in its haste to share in the material fruits of industrial progress, was selling its birthright. The capitulation to Northern industrialism was particularly stultifying to the artist. As Donald Davidson said: "The Southern tradition in which these writers would share has been discredited and made artistically inaccessible; . . . One has to look closely at the provincial Southern artists to discover traces of the indigenous Southern."[31]

In 1930 after much discussion and debate, four of the Fugitives—Ransom, Davidson, Tate, and Warren—joined eight other Southerners in writing *I'll Take My Stand* (1930), a collection of essays in support of a Southern way of life "against what may be called the American or prevailing way." All twelve Southerners subscribed to a prefatory "Statement of Principles," a catalogue of the ills of industrialism written by Ransom and crystallizing the distinction between the two ways of life in the phrase "Agrarian *versus* Industrial."[32] From Oxford, Warren sent an essay entitled "The Briar Patch," a discussion of the race question and a defense of segregation.

Characteristically, Warren treats the subject historically, briefly tracing the stages by which the South—and the North—reached the present dilemma. The panacea he offers is gradualism, the mutual and patient education of both Negroes and whites; for the problem of the poor and illiterate Negro is inextricable from the problem of the poor and illiterate white. Warren aligns himself with the general economic and political tenor of *I'll Take My Stand* by pointing out that the tendency of industrialism to intensify competition and to uproot the Negro from his traditional and accustomed role on the farm will exacerbate the situation. The argument, however, is not without its contradiction. Warren has faith in education, but he knows that good education is expensive and that the South is poor. Consequently, "the increasing prosperity of the section may give considerable hope for the future." The Northern reader, smarting under the attack on his system, would be quick to note that such prosperity as the South enjoys is that based on the despised industrialism. Fundamentally, however, Warren sees the problem as a moral one: "What the white workman must learn, and his education may be as long and laborious as the negro's, is that he may respect himself as a white man, but, if he fails to concede the negro equal protection, he does not properly respect himself as a man" (260).

As a result of Warren's short-lived connection with the Agrarians, he has been repeatedly associated with a socio-economic thesis which his later work in part repudiates and ultimately transcends. While in sympathy with the broad humanistic aims of the contributors to *I'll Take My Stand,* he doubted the wisdom of the title and wished to call the book *Tracts Against Communism.* Nor, in retrospect, did he feel satisfied with his treatment of the race problem. "I remember," he said later, "the jangle and wrangle of writing the essay and some kind of discomfort in it, some sense of evasion."[33] As for his argument, the need for the establishment of "an informed and productive negro community," the forces for social justice unleashed since World War II have rendered it obsolete. As a temporary expedient for its time, it was sensible enough. As Warren said, "There wasn't a power under heaven that could have changed segregation in 1929—the South wasn't ready for it, the North wasn't ready for it, the Negro wasn't."[34] But personally, Warren has completely reversed his earlier position. After pondering the problem for a number of years, Warren undertook a trip in 1956 through the section of the South he had known best—Kentucky, Tennessee, Arkansas, Mississippi, and Louisiana—the result of which was his long essay: *Segregation: The Inner Conflict in the South.*

This book is a superb piece of journalism, a report of conversations the author had with Southerners and with himself. It is an eminently temperate and wise consideration of the race situation in the South. Without editorializing and without rancor, Warren dramatically builds up, in a wide-ranging dialogue between Negro and white, a picture of the daily humiliations that segregation imposes on both the oppressor and the oppressed. In contrast to his treatment of the question in "The Briar Patch," Warren clearly sounds the moral imperative. Segregation is not, however, a question of abstract morality; "it has to be solved in a context for possible solutions" (113). And the essential problem is not "to learn to live with the Negro. It is to learn to live with ourselves" (111). If nothing else, *Segregation* reveals the complex domestic implications of the race question in the South. And at the heart of the matter is the pervasive and paradoxical sense of community that we have already seen as the seedbed of the Southern Literary Renaissance. Warren, probing the motives for segregation, crystallizes this sense of community in two brief conversations.

> Pridefulness, money, level of intelligence, race, God's will, filth and disease, power, hate, contempt, legality—perhaps these are not all the words that get mentioned. There is another thing, whatever the word for it. An eminent Negro scholar is, I suppose, saying something about the other thing. "One thing," he says, "is that a lot of people down here just don't like change. It's not merely desegregation they're against so much, it's just the fact of any change. They feel some emotional tie to the way things are. A change is disorienting, especially if you're pretty disoriented already." . . . And I hear a college student in the Deep South: "You know, it's just that people don't like to feel they're spitting on their grandfather's grave. They feel some connection they don't want to break. Something would bother them if they broke it."
>
> The young man is, I gather, an integrationist. He adds: "And sometimes something bothers them if they don't break it."
>
> Let us give a name now to whatever it is that the eminent Negro scholar and the young white college boy were talking about. Let us, without meaning to be ironical, call it piety.
>
> (55-56)

Warren understands this paradox at the center of Southern life, this powerful sense of history that at once vitalizes and vitiates life in the South. It is a constant tension in his own writing, and it is his awareness of its significance that drew him for a season into the camp of the Agrarians. In 1956 the Fugitives reassembled at Vanderbilt University for a reunion. The talk turned to a consideration of the Agrarian movement and its ultimate meaning both for the United States and for the men who sponsored it. "For me," Warren said, "it was a protest . . . against a kind of de-humanizing and disintegrative effect on your notion of what an individual person could be. . . . The past is always a rebuke to the present; . . . It's a better rebuke than any dream of the future. It's a better rebuke because you can see what some of the costs were, what frail virtues were achieved in the past by frail men."[35]

V

Warren returned from Oxford in 1930 to begin his career as a teacher of English. He spent a year at Southwestern College in Memphis, moving on the following year to his alma mater, Vanderbilt. In 1934, he joined the English department at Louisiana State University, just as the flamboyant Huey Long, then at the height of his power, was lavishing money and attention on the university.

Much has been written of the dangers of Academe to the creative writer. Warren himself has dissected the stifling atmosphere of the small college in two short stories. "The Life and Work of Professor Roy Millan" is a scathing study of a man whose soul has been withered by the niggling economies and pathetic self-deceptions that compose life in a small, rural college. Similarly, the central character in "The Unvexed Isles," Professor Dalrymple, has found the role of college teacher an escape upward from a boyhood of dirt farms and poverty into the rigid hierarchy of Southern gentility. Both stories are primarily studies in atmosphere, evoking the pallid and pretentious community of the rural college, tense with the strain of preserving appearances and vitiated by small vanities and petty jealousies.

However, Warren's own career and his comments on the teaching profession contradict the testimony of his fiction. In 1939, after a decade of academic life, he concluded that in general it was helpful: "For a person who wants to write, the advantages of teaching, I believe, outweigh the disadvantages; a teacher is forced to clarify—or to try to clarify—his own mind on certain questions which are necessarily involved in the business of writing."[36] A decade later his opinion was unchanged: "There are very fundamental compensations in teaching if you're in the right kind of place and have the right kind of students. . . . A university has the failures and defects of institutions, just like government or the family or anything else. But I do think it gives certain perspectives in its better reaches that you'd not get if you were outside."[37]

Although Warren's career as a classroom teacher has been a dedicated and distinguished one, he has not allowed it to absorb all of his energies. That those energies are prodigious may easily be seen by chronicling his other activities during his years at Louisiana State University. In addition to teaching three courses, he was writing with Cleanth Brooks, his colleague in the English department, two influential textbooks, *Understanding Poetry* (1938) and *Understanding Fiction* (1943). To these labors were added, after 1935, a staggering amount of work connected with the founding and editing of the *Southern Review*.

The founding of this review was totally unexpected and apparently casual.[38] Its genesis was a Sunday afternoon call in February, 1935, by the president of the university, James Monroe Smith, in the course of which he invited Warren to edit a literary and critical quarterly to be supported by university funds. Warren, with Cleanth Brooks and another Vanderbilt alumnus, Charles W. Pipkin, accepted the challenge; and during the next seven years they edited the journal which Ray B. West, Jr., has called "the most highly respected literary journal in America during the 1930's."[39] The tables of contents glitter with illustrious names: Herbert Agar, W. H. Auden, Kenneth Burke, T. S. Eliot, Ford Madox Ford, Caroline Gordon, Aldous Huxley, Katherine Anne Porter, John Crowe Ransom, Wallace Stevens, Allen Tate, and Mark Van Doren. The editors had a gift for spotting new talent as well, and the *Southern Review* sponsored the early work of such writers as Nelson Algren, R. P. Blackmur, Randall Jarrell, Mary McCarthy, F. O. Matthiessen, Delmore Schwartz, Theodore Spenser, and Eudora Welty.

The purpose of the magazine was to contribute to the cultural life of the South, and the editors, naturally enough, hoped it would become the focal point of that life. The title itself was an expression, as they said, "of the regional and sectional piety of the editors."[40] There was, however, a conscious desire to avoid any taint of provincialism or chauvinism. No attempt was made to limit the contributions to those from the South or to insist on local color in subject matter or regional consciousness in treatment. Eventually the magazine had a list of contributors and a circulation that belied any charge of parochialism. It reached a circulation of approximately fifteen hundred, concentrated in the middle South, the North-East, and the West Coast. An encouraging number of subscriptions came from England, and, as the editors observed, their lists included more readers in Calcutta and Tokyo than in Atlanta, Georgia.

In 1942 the publication was suspended by order of the president of the university. There were a number of reasons for its demise. Several members of the faculty were hostile, and certain officers of the administration felt that, during wartime, the journal was a luxury the university could not afford. Others had been critical of the magazine as unrealistic and remote from the fundamental concerns of a university. With the suspension of the magazine, Warren left Louisiana State to take a position as professor of English and director of the creative writing program at the University of Minnesota.

Warren's appointment to the new post calls attention to another concern, in fact the central concern, which had occupied him while teaching in the South. Throughout these years, as he said, "my deep and abiding desire was to write poetry and fiction, and even though I felt no competition between this desire and the profession I enjoyed, I turned most of my energy, when I left the classroom and the obligations of the classroom, toward writing poems and stories and novels."[41] Warren had published a number of short stories during the 1930's, and he had in progress a novel dealing with the world of his Kentucky boyhood. But because the writing of verse had been his absorbing interest since Fugitive days, it is to a consideration of the achievement of his early poetry that we must first turn.

CHAPTER 2

The Texture of the World

IN THE SPRING of 1943 Robert Penn Warren published in the *Kenyon Review* an essay entitled "Pure and Impure Poetry" which has since taken its place among the major texts of modern criticism. Warren himself evidently believed the essay constituted an important personal statement, for he subsequently placed it first in his *Selected Essays* (1958). Since the essay appeared while he was preparing his *Selected Poems, 1923-1943* for the press, he was perhaps prompted to speculate on the nature of poetry by looking back on two decades of his own practice of the art.

"Poetry," Warren begins, "wants to be pure but poems do not." The poet writing the pure poem is, like the laboratory scientist, working under carefully controlled conditions to extract the emotion pure and undefiled. The pure poem is the distillate, the emotion purged of the dross of ambiguity. Warren insists, however, that the poem must have its being not in the aseptic laboratory but in the world. Consequently, the poem must, like life itself, partake of impurities: "cacophonies, jagged rhythms, ugly words and ugly thoughts, colloquialisms, clichés, sterile technical terms, headwork, and argument, self-contradictions, clevernesses, irony, realism—all things which call us back to the world of prose and imperfection." If, for example, the pure poet (Warren's examples are Shelley and Tennyson) treats of love, he is likely to represent it as ethereal and beautiful and pure. Love is for him a "soft" subject, and he will insist on its "softness." But, Warren argues, it is just this insistence which leads to the downfall of the pure poet. Love may be bawdy and sensual and comic. If the poem does not contain some awareness of this paradoxical nature of love, some ironic counterstatement, the poem is vulnerable to parody and ridicule. The result may be an "embarrassing" poem or a "naked" poem. Warren's ideal poet "is like the jujitsu expert; he wins by utilizing the resistance of his opponent—the materials of the poem. In other words, a poem, to be good, must earn itself."

In terms of his own definition, Warren's poetry is decidedly impure. From his first verses, written while still an undergraduate at Vanderbilt, he has readily introduced into his poetry all of the elements so troubling to the pure poet. Warren employs, for example, a remarkable variety of metrical forms, often in startling combinations. Sudden contrasts between elegance and earthiness abound in his verse—the coupling of a Latinic adjective and an Anglo-Saxon noun and the mixing of esoteric diction with slang. The folk speech of his native Kentucky and Tennessee is a Warren hallmark, his ear for dialect going beyond mere quirks of vocabulary or oddities of syntax. In its system of tensions, his poetry harks back to the elaborately fashioned and intellectually rigorous verse of the decidedly impure Metaphysicals. The result is a poetry of tartness and astringency which lays him open to the charge that has been made against his former teacher and fellow Fugitive, John Crowe Ransom—a deficiency in verbal music.

Warren was undoubtedly influenced by Ransom, as was an entire generation of Southern poets. Ransom's students include Donald Davidson, Allen Tate, Andrew Lytle, Randall Jarrell, and Robert Lowell. "Perhaps," Robert Lowell has said, "their being with Ransom was an irrelevant accident. And yet, I think the teacher may have made the difference."[1] In "Pure and Impure Poetry" Warren pays high tribute to Ransom by including at the center of the essay an admiring explication of the metrical brilliance and ironic wit of "Bells for John Whiteside's Daughter."[2] Ransom, on his part, has called Warren "one of the really superlative poets of our time."[3]

During the two years he was associated with the Fugitives, Warren published more than a score of poems in their magazine. "Crusade," his first poem to be accepted for publication, appeared in the number for June, 1923, and in February, 1924, his name was added to the masthead of the magazine. While his poems do not appear to disadvantage beside the work others were contributing, Warren's verses are not remarkably superior to those of many talented young people whose interest in literature stimulates them to write poetry. Generally traditional in form, these early poems are characterized by a fascination with the macabre and the monstrous. Warren's imagination seems to have been haunted by images of putrefaction and disease. Death is everywhere, generally at its most hideous—"naked corpses," "skulls glaring white," "flies on bloated bodies," in a world of "leprous" mists, "shriveling" ferns, and "obscene" wheat. There are clear echoes of T. S. Eliot, particularly the emotional stance of "J. Alfred Prufrock" and the hard precision and abrupt transitions of "Gerontion." The tone is melodramatic, a turgid and overwrought straining for effect. Only when Warren turns to material he knows intimately, notably in the poignant lyric elegy "Alf Burt, Tenant Farmer," do we catch glimpses of real promise.

After his graduation from Vanderbilt in 1925, Warren spent the summer revising and polishing these early poems for publication. He told Allen Tate that he had about thirty-eight in his portfolio, but that he had "few illusions about them."[4] Ultimately he determined against publication, and another decade was to pass before he brought out in 1935 his first volume of verse under the title *Thirty-Six Poems.*

In preparing the volume for the press, Warren winnowed out much of his early work. The only poem that survives from undergraduate days is "To a Face in a Crowd," which had appeared in the *Fugitive* (June, 1925) and was later included in *Fugitives: An Anthology of Verse* (1928). The poem, clearly the best of his earlier work, is representative of it in tone and theme. The form is traditional four-line, iambic pentameter stanzas;

the mood is Eliotic. As the title suggests, the poem is a plea for communion with a stranger whose "face is blown, an apparition, past." The setting is a place of "bitter waters" where "among the rocks the faint lascivious grass/Fingers in lust the arrogant bones of men." The speaker feels that he has seen the face before, perhaps in a dream. He can address the stranger as "my brother," for together they share a dark and violent history which they have no choice but to confront. The speaker knows, too, that such tenuous communion as is possible between them must be based on a recognition of their common past.

> . . . we must meet
> As weary nomads in this desert at last,
> Borne in the lost procession of these feet.

I

The contents of *Thirty-Six Poems* show great strides beyond the derivative, artificial verses of Warren's Fugitive period. In his essay on Robert Frost, Warren has defined the poet as "the man who is greatly concerned with the flux of things, with the texture of the world, with, even, the dark 'natural' places of man's soul."[5] So it is with Warren's own poems. His work confronts the elemental facts of human experience, and yet, as might be expected, it is deeply rooted in his native region. "The Last Metaphor" and "Croesus in Autumn," for example, offer frequent glimpses of Kentucky landscape, vivid with precisely observed and sharply focused images. This deeply felt sense of place never descends into mere local color but is the wellspring of the poetry's vitality. The predominant mood is autumnal: falling leaves, the sound of wind in barren boughs, "the scent of the year's declension." The poetry is suffused with a sense of natural forces at work—the cycle of the seasons, the generations of men, the flow of time.

A case in point is the series of seven lyrics written between 1927 and 1932 and grouped under the title "Kentucky Mountain Farm." Two poems in this sequence, "The Cardinal" and "The

Jay," are as eloquently lyrical as anything Warren has written. In the opening "Rebuke of the Rocks," the rocks address the "little stubborn people of the hill," instructing them that the "little flesh and fevered bone/May keep the sweet sterility of stone." But even the rocks are at the mercy of massive natural processes, for

> the frost has torn
> Away their ridgéd fundaments at last,
> So that the fractured atoms now are borne
> Down shifting waters to the tall, profound
> Shadow of the absolute deeps, . . .

In "History Among the Rocks" the speaker wonders about the young soldiers, "grey coats, blue coats," slaughtered on the very mountainside where the farm now stands. He reflects on the ways a man may die: freezing in winter snow, drowning in a spring flood, poisoning by a copperhead while harvesting summer wheat. The violence inherent in each way of dying is muted by the poet's treatment. Freezing to death is but "a cold and crystalline dream"; the drowned man is "hushed in the end" as the waters "gently bend." Considered against the cycle of the year, such deaths are but the course of nature, the inevitable risks of life. By contrast, "Young men on the mountainside/Clambered, fought. Heels muddied the rocky spring." The men sought death in "these autumn orchards." They fought furiously, died violently, and their deaths seem somehow to violate the natural order. The speaker is puzzled by their motives.

> Their reason is hard to guess, remembering
> Blood on their black mustaches in moonlight.
> Their reason is hard to guess and a long time past:
> The apple falls, falling in the quiet night.

The ending is a characteristic Warren signature. The final image is cryptic, at most an oblique suggestion of the meaning of the experience described in the poem. Compared to the men killed by natural calamities, the soldiers have consciously chosen to court death. Perhaps it is the exercise of this choice that lends dignity and meaning to their lives. The poet does not say; he merely points to the fall of the apple, an image suggesting the vast natural forces at work in the universe against which the soldiers' decision must be measured.

Among these early poems we find the first tentative exploration of themes and techniques which Warren returns to and develops in his later poetry and fiction. The flippant, slangy idiom of "Pondy Woods" looks forward to the speech of Duckfoot Blake in *At Heaven's Gate* and Jack Burden in *All the King's Men.* "Letter of a Mother" and "The Return: An Elegy" are preliminary sketches for one of the most familiar narrative patterns of Warren's later work.[6] Each dramatizes, by a cycle of flight and return, the mingled feelings of love, responsibility and guilt between a mother and her son. The son, driven by a dimly felt need for self-realization, flees the family homestead only to be haunted by a nagging sense of filial obligation.

In "The Return," the best of Warren's early work, we hear the first confident sounding of his characteristic poetic voice. The elegy develops, as a number of commentators have noted,[7] by a series of violent shifts in tone. The speaker is hurrying westward to the bedside of his dying mother. In the darkness the pines whip past the Pullman window, stimulating in the son's mind a chain of grotesque and irreverent associations. The glimpses of Southern landscape, swept by rain squalls and low-hanging mists, merge with childhood memories, speculations on the pioneers who first made the journey westward, and sudden and uncontrollable spasms of guilt ("the old bitch is dead/what have I said!"). The speaker imagines, or remembers, a dead fox lying amidst ferns and blossoms, and his imagination clothes the scene in the formal trappings of a funeral ("the gracious catafalque and pall"). His mind irrationally metamorphoses the memory of the fox into the memory of his mother ("the old fox is dead/what have I said"). Images rise in the mind, combine and recombine, in a disconnected series of soaring leaps and tangents. Scraps of verse are blended with memories after the manner of Eliot's *Waste Land*:

> turn backward turn backward in your flight
> and make me a child again just for tonight
> good lord he's wet the bed come bring a light

The kaleidoscopic images blur and eddy in the speaker's mind and build to the memorable conclusion:

> If I could pluck
> Out of the dark that whirled
> Over the hoarse pine over the rock
> Out of the mist that furled
> Could I stretch forth like God the hand and gather
> For you my mother
> If I could pluck
> Against the dry essential of tomorrow
> To lay upon the breast that gave me suck
> Out of the dark the dark and swollen orchid of this sorrow.

These lines recapitulate the dominant imagery of the poem and rise to the intensity of the final metaphor which precisely defines the son's sense of loss.

"The Return" is almost a parable of a special kind of Southern experience in the twentieth century. The narrator has fled the region of his birth, yet has felt the past sucking him down like quicksand. He is hard put to define the ambivalence of his attitude toward the South. In part, his is the plight of the deracinated intellectual; in part, the plight of a man attempting to come to terms with his personal past.

Warren's continuing concern with the theme of the past in the present gives special significance to his poem "History." His use of a flexible but firmly controlled rhyme scheme and of jagged, broken rhythms gives the poem a taut, sinewy power. At nightfall the narrator, an invader of a foreign land, stands at the head of a pass in a mountain defile looking down upon a verdant and fertile plain. On the verge of triumph, he recalls the advance through a bleak and barren wasteland. The army was confused and exhausted, but morale remained high. The intensity of the struggle, the concentration on the "prophesied" goal had given life meaning and direction. Now, poised at the moment of victory, the narrator pauses to speculate on his place in history and on the sons who will come after him:

> Our sons shall cultivate
> Peculiar crimes,
> Having not love, nor hate
> Nor memory.
> Though some,
> Of all most weary,
> Most defective of desire,
> Shall grope toward time's cold womb;
> In dim pools peer
> To see, of some grandsire,
> The long and toothèd jawbone greening there.

The dilemma described is that of a generation of men paralyzed by their spiritual vacuity. For their ancestors, time offered an opportunity for action. For themselves, time is

> the aimless bitch . . .
> Forever quartering the ground in which
> The blank and fanged
> Rough certainty lies hid.

The invader, ruminating on the search for meaning which will occupy his progeny, suddenly asks himself what is the motive of his own quest:

> We seek what end?
> The slow dynastic ease,
> Travail's cease?
> Not pleasure, sure:
> Alloy of fact?
> The act
> Alone is pure.

Submerged in the life of action, he finds the act self-justifying and self-fulfilling.

The diction and imagery of "History" carry overtones of the Israelites girding themselves to conquer the Promised Land, but the poem is distinctly contemporary in mood. The Israelite descending into the Promised Land is an allegory of the modern condition and a commentary on the American Dream. The emigrant to the New World, redeemed in action, has been replaced by the alienated modern who ransacks the past for direction and is baffled by the multiplicity of its meanings.

Closely related to "History" in their contemporaneity are two poems, companion pieces, published by Warren in the *Southern Review* (July, 1935) and included in *Thirty-Six Poems*. Both mirror the unrest of the depression years and both are grimly prophetic. The first of these, "Ransom," points to the perilous uncertainty of the times: "What wars and lecheries and the old zeal/Yet unfulfilled, unrarefied, unlaced." The poem goes on to state a problem: "Our courage needs, perhaps, new definition"; the second poem, "Letter from a Coward to a Hero," offers one solution.

The "letter" opens with a fragmented account of the hero's day, a trivial mixture of blemished triumphs and minor disappointments that make up even the days of heroes. The writer catalogues the events and adds simply: "I think you deserved better;/Therefore I am writing you this letter." The self-confessed coward muses on the childhood he shared with the hero, scraps of memory which "are hard to reconstruct," probing for the sources of the hero's strength. The writer is aware that the time is out of joint and that he is inadequate to its demands:

> Guns blaze in autumn and
> The quail falls and
> Empires collide with a bang
> That shakes the pictures where they hang
> And democracy shows signs of dry rot . . .
> But a good hunter holds the point
> And is not gun-shy;
> But I
> Am gun-shy.

The attitude of the coward toward the hero is touched with ambiguity. Though kingdoms totter and the skies fall, the hero, like the obedient hunting dog, holds the point. The comparison is calculated to flatter only the most complacent of heroes. Such courage is a virtue, but not an unalloyed one; for it is an unthinking courage, rather like a conditioned reflex.

The writer, moreover, is troubled by thoughts of the future. He hears "Drums beating for/The big war." He asks nervously, "Does the airman scream in the flaming trajectory?" He knows that the future will call for men of heroic mold, but he is concerned about the hero's qualifications. The writer continues with a stanza that defines more exactly his attitude toward the hero:

> You have been strong in love and hate.
> Disaster owns less speed than you have got,
> But he will cut across the back lot
> To lurk and lie in wait.
> Admired of children, gathered for their games,
> Disaster, like the dandelion, blooms,
> And the delicate film is fanned
> To seed the shaven lawn.

The relationship delineated is infinitely more subtle than the polarized terms *coward* and *hero* suggest. The hero, the speaker tells us, is swift and, in the race with Disaster, possesses superior speed but inferior cunning. Disaster is wily and may outwit even the strongest of heroes. Disaster's seeds are sown as casually and abundantly as those of wild flowers and may take root in the most carefully cultivated places. Like a child playing with matches, the hero plays with Disaster, oblivious to the possible consequences of his actions. The writer of the letter frankly admires the hero's courage, but his admiration is tempered by the quality of that courage. It is too innocent, too abstract. Thus, in "Letter From a Coward to a Hero" we have the first extended poetic statement of a compelling theme which Warren first explored in his biography of John Brown: the man untroubled by self-knowledge who brings disaster by his single-minded devotion to an abstract virtue.

A similar problem is treated in a more traditional form in one of Warren's most appealing lyrics, "The Garden," a variation on a theme by Andrew Marvell. Marvell in his great poem describes a verdant garden at the height of summer, but Warren describes a garden in early autumn when the first frost has dimmed its "summered brilliance." Now, with summer's blossoms gone, the leaves blaze with "stately flame" and the trees echo with the song of jay and cardinal. The speaker, pondering on the garden's earlier state when it was a "rank plot" of lush ripeness, imagines two lovers pausing in an arbor before they kiss, "instructed of what ripeness is." Perhaps these lovers are Adam and Eve, for as in Marvell's poem, the garden here carries suggestions of the Garden of Eden. It is an "imperial" yet natural garden ("No marbles whitely gaze among/These paths"). The sun is a "benison" and the narrator feels that "these precincts wait/In sacrament."

Marvell's garden is paradisaical; in it man may recapture something of the innocence and spiritual wholeness he enjoyed before the Fall. Warren's garden, on the other hand, is the "ruined state" after the Fall; in it man can find not innocence but knowledge. Thus the Fall (punning on the season) is, paradoxically, a fortunate one, for from the knowledge gained of the grossness of human excess and of the power of nature for evil, man may forge a new sacramental innocence on which to be stayed. The significance for Warren of the theme of "The Garden"—that only by knowledge does man achieve his identity—may be surmised by the fact that two decades after writing the poem he restated (in a speech in 1954 at Columbia University) the theme using the same imagery: "Man can return to his lost unity, and if that return is fitful and precarious, if the foliage and flower of the innocent garden are now somewhat browned by a late season, all is the more precious for the fact, for what is now achieved has been achieved by a growth of moral awareness."

II

Having explored the theme of the loss of innocence and the hope of redemption through knowledge in "The Garden," Warren turned to a more extended treatment of it in *Eleven Poems on the Same Theme,* one of "The Poet of the Month" series brought out by New Directions in 1942. This slender pamphlet, the product of a mind steeped in the tradition of English poetry, is unique in the Warren canon, for nowhere else is his great range and intellectual force displayed with so much economy and intensity. In "Bearded Oaks," for example, Warren handles the lyric quatrain with a sensitive feeling for the traditional form yet with a startling originality of execution.

The dense texture of "Love's Parable," with its staccato rhythms and faintly archaic diction, blends wit and imagination after the manner of the Metaphysicals. The dialectic of "Question and Answer" is worked out in a taut but expressive free verse. The rigorous discipline of the individual poems extends to the organization of the work as a whole. Fugal in structure, it is developed and enriched by each new variation on the central theme. *Eleven Poems* is further integrated by recurring imagery —sun and sea, light and dark, stone and bone—which gives an inner logic to poems widely disparate in formal structure.

The theme of the eleven poems is stated metaphorically in the lyric that opens the volume, "Monologue at Midnight." In it innocence is equated with love, and knowledge with disillusion. The speaker wishes to define himself in relation to another whom he loved and with whom he shared "joy and innocence" and "simplicity." Their love was as fresh as the green of the cathedral pines that sheltered it and as natural as the progress of the seasons against which it unfolded. These memories of innocence are contaminated by the intrusion of vague overtones of guilt. Images, insubstantial and incongruous, flash into the mind of the narrator: the lovers' shadows guiltily pursuing them, an echo carried by the night wind, the sudden spurt of a match which fitfully and faintly promises a moment of illumination. The narrator can find neither substance nor definition ("And which am I and which are you?") and concludes with a muted plea for spiritual wholeness and integration of self: "Our mathematic yet has use/For the integers of blessedness." His isolation and sense of loss are acute, and he is only groping toward the formulation of the insight which Warren voices in "Revelation" and which, in turn, becomes one of the controlling themes of his later poetry and fiction: "In separateness only does love learn definition."

By contrast, "Bearded Oaks," the poem that follows, describes a moment of fulfillment, a moment poised precariously beyond the claims of time with its inevitable involvements and contamination. Two lovers recline in a grove of oaks. To the narrator the scene appears submerged in water with light filtering down through layers of liquid darkness. All motion is slowed by the denser medium, and, in this retardation of movement, the speaker feels time itself suspended. The lovers themselves are "twin atolls." In the depths only faint whispers reach them of worldly processes, emphasizing the intense stillness of the present moment and its withdrawal from time's action of "passion and slaughter, ruth, decay . . ." The apparent serenity of the scene prompts the narrator to sound a positive note: "If hope is hopeless, then fearless fear/And history is thus undone." Yet even this guarded and tentative assertion is rendered ironic by the illusory nature of the setting.

The submarine imagery of the scene—its suspension, as it were, in both water and time—is evoked by the languid quality of the verse with its heavily marked caesuras, its stately progression of sonorous open vowels, and its inversions which force a marked slowing of pace:

> The oaks, how subtle and marine,
> Bearded, and all the layered light
> Above them swims; and thus the scene,
> Recessed, awaits the positive night.
>
> So, waiting, we in the grass now lie
> Beneath the langorous tread of light:
> The grasses, kelp-like, satisfy
> The nameless motions of the air.

The elegance of "Bearded Oaks" is sustained in "Picnic Remembered" and "Love's Parable." Although structurally and metrically more formal than the other pieces in *Eleven Poems,* both lyrics extend and develop the thematic material and the imagery. In "Picnic Remembered," as in "Bearded Oaks," the lovers are suspended outside of time like "twin flies, . . . in amber tamed." The day appears "innocent" to the lovers "buoyed" like swimmers who "resign them to the flow/And pause of their unstained flood." But the sunlight which "laved" them is deceptive, for their innocence is ignorance: "we did not know/How darkness darker staired below." Similarly, in "Love's Parable" the lover rejoices in a "garden state of innocence" only to have all spoiled by the "inward sore of self."

Reading sequentially through *Eleven Poems,* it is not until we come to "Original Sin: A Short Story" that we reach the finest example of an idiom that Warren has made unmistakably his own. The apparent colloquial ease is achieved by piling up circumstantial details after the manner of a gifted, if rather garrulous, raconteur. The images are often macabre ("seaweed strung on the stinking stone") and the humor sardonic or cynical ("grandpa's will paid the ticket"). Abstractions ("the quantum glare of sun") are set off against folk speech ("riding the rods"). The five-stress, iambic line is shaped and ordered by a traditional rhyme scheme, but the pattern is varied by the frequent spondees and anapests and by the use of slant rhymes.

"Original Sin" reads, as John M. Bradbury has said, "like a tightly condensed and highly figurative version of a Warren novel."[8] Warren himself has given us a clue to the poem's intended meaning: "The story is about the personal past and the past behind the personal past, I suppose, and the problem that contemplating this past makes for us in our world of mobility and disorientation."[9] The protagonist is in flight, in part from his own past; in part, from some aspect of himself connected with that past which he cannot bring himself to face. It may be, as the poem's title suggests, man's innate depravity. Restlessly searching for "a new innocence . . . to be stayed by," the protagonist cannot elude the old guilt which reappears remorselessly in a variety of guises—a nightmare, an old hound, the clock steeple in Harvard Yard. These isolated but vivid images from youth are loosed from the depths of memory and float upward into consciousness to define an apparently forgotten experience. For example,

> . . . your grandpa, who
> Had a wen on his forehead and sat on the veranda
> To finger the precious protuberance, as was his habit to do,
> Which glinted in sun like rough garnet or the rich old brain
>   bulging through.

The speaker has more than once felt the elation of escaping from the protean and dreaded visitant; but, just at the moment his defenses are down, it reappears. At the end, the speaker becomes accommodated to a sort of self-irony. He is apparently reconciled to the now familiar experience and even finds a gloomy kind of satisfaction in the assurance that "it" will continue to haunt him.

The protagonist in "Crime," unlike the central figure in "Original Sin," has escaped the past, but insanity is the price he has had to pay for his release. The burden of guilt has become intolerable: "He cannot seem to remember . . . he is too tired to ask . . . He cannot say . . ." The poem is an excursion into the psychology of insanity: the horrors of a diseased imagination where a tree is a "sibilant tumor," where "walls confer in the silent house," and where "eyes of pictures protrude, like a snail's, each on its prong." Yet "Crime" does not violate the thematic integrity of the volume as a whole. The killer has buried a body under the leaves, but he has forgotten the act and the victim. We are told to "envy the mad killer" because he too searches for happiness and "peace in God's eye"; his burden of guilt, unlike ours, is expiated in violence and madness. For the sane, even in an insane society, the burden remains; for "memory drips, a pipe in the cellar dark."

In "Pursuit" Warren confronts directly the issue of the disruption of the modern sensibility. Warren has defined the problem in the course of a discussion of the poetry of John Crowe Ransom:[10]

> The disruption of sensibility . . . has two aspects: man is a creature little lower than the angels and, at the same time, of the brute creation; again, there is a conflict between the scientific vision of quantity and that vision concerned with quality. The issue in itself is as old as man, but in the past a reconciliation has generally been possible in terms provided by a more stable way of life and a more ordered structure of ideas. The issue receives its contemporary poignancy by reason of the absence of those two things. . . . The issue is the source of Ransom's irony. The poet cannot solve his problem by an act of will, but he can attempt to work out some sort of equilibrium that may permit him, even though at odds with himself, to continue the practice of his art without violating his own honesty.

Warren's own treatment of the issue in "Pursuit" is also ironic. The pursuit is more an escape into sensation and a flight from the satiety of self. The stanzas proceed by a kind of dialectic, a series of contrasts at once grotesque and romantic. The pervasive tone of illness is encountered at once in the opening reference to a hunchback who harbors his own secrets and, like a victorious general, stares silently at "you" with "imperious innocence." The "you" of the poem is in part the generalized reader, but it is also one voice of a schizoid modern self, a rather petulant and censorious super-ego.

The second stanza of "Pursuit" speaks in the imperative mood: "Go to the clinic. Wait in the outer room." As in the contrast of hunchback and general, the sick modern is compared to the barbarian conqueror of imperial Rome who gapes uneasily at the undaunted sacrificial fathers. But compared to the richness of the allusion, the modern man is incapable of an adequate or appropriate emotional response to his own plight and feels merely "like one who has come too late, or improperly clothed, to a party." A similar contrast develops in the third stanza. A doctor, baffled by the patient whose symptoms he cannot interpret, prescribes a trip to Florida where the frivolous search for diversion of the hypochondriac contrasts strikingly with the heroic quest of Ponce de Leon.

The modern disjunction of feeling and intellect is distilled in the conceit which opens the fifth stanza: "In Florida consider the flamingo,/Its color passion but its neck a question." And finally, as in "Original Sin," the problem revolves around the difficulty of contemplating the past: "Solution, perhaps, is public, despair personal,/But history held to your breath clouds like a mirror."

"Terror," the poem that concludes *Eleven Poems,* is quite similar to "Pursuit." Warren has given us an account of the circumstances of its composition.[11] While spending the winter of 1939-40 in Rome on a Guggenheim grant, Warren's attention was caught by a news item in the Rome daily *Il Messaggero* announcing that United States volunteers serving in the Finnish forces then fighting Russia would not lose their citizenship.

The same morning he came upon the report of the death of the chicken heart which Alexis Carrel had kept alive in his laboratory and which the sensational press had exploited in stories promising earthly immortality.

> The business about the chicken heart [Warren wrote] seemed to summarize a view current in our time—that science (as popularly conceived) will solve the problem of evil by reducing it merely to a matter of "adjustment" in the physical, social, economic, and political spheres. That same day I recalled a remark made in some book by John Strachey that after science had brought "adjustment" to society it would then solve the problem of evil by bringing man a mortal immortality, by abolishing disease and death. It struck me as somewhat strange that Strachey should equate physical death and evil on a point-to-point basis, and should thereby imply that good and physical survival are identical. As for the report about the volunteers, I was struck by the thought that the same impulse which had made them go to fight Franco had made them go to fight Russia, their recent ally in Spain. That impulse officially manifested itself as a political idea, a solution for the problem of meaning in life in terms of "adjustment," but, for the purposes of the poem at least, I take a large component of that impulse to be the *passionate emptiness and tidal lust* of the modern man who, because he cannot find long-range meaning, seeks meaning in mere violence, the violence being what he wants and needs without reference ultimately to the political or other justification he may appeal to. So the two reports set us a paradox: the yearning for mere survival as meaning, and the appetite for death as meaning.

The poem addresses "you," the modern man, who has been "born to no adequate definition of terror." His plight is that, blind alike to his limitations and responsibilities, he seeks restlessly to allay a gnawing, spiritual hunger. Yet nothing satisfies, neither the pleasure of the coldly passionate intellect nor the lust for physical sensation. Since Warren was living in Rome during the composition of the poem, he was following at close quarters the efforts of Hitler and Mussolini to carve up Europe. Hence the allusions of "Terror" have a topicality not generally found in *Eleven Poems*:

> You know, by radio, how hotly the world repeats,
> When the brute crowd roars or the blunt boot-heels resound
> In the Piazza or the Wilhelmplatz, . . .

Warren has commented on the political content of the poem: "Nazism, Fascism, embody . . . the glorification of violence and death, the offer of salvation through practical success, adjustment, etc., the 'rational' state. But the boot-heels beating the stones in the Piazza or Wilhelmplatz set up echoes of the same impulses and desires across the Atlantic—all part of the same world, the same modernity."[12]

III

In the winter of 1944 Robert Penn Warren brought out his *Selected Poems, 1923-1943*. This collection is made up substantially of the poems which had already appeared in *Thirty-Six Poems* and in *Eleven Poems on the Same Theme*. There is, however, one important addition, "The Ballad of Billie Potts," a long and ambitious work which Warren placed first in the new edition.

For the student of Warren's work, "The Ballad of Billie Potts" is of absorbing interest, notwithstanding the fact that as a work of art it is gravely flawed. In its composition Warren set himself a problem of great difficulty—dramatizing the meaning of the past for the present. Warren's continuing efforts to solve this problem to his own satisfaction have prompted his finest work: the two novels *All the King's Men* and *World Enough and Time* and his long narrative poem *Brother to Dragons*.

The subject of the ballad is drawn from the folk history of Warren's home country—a story, he tells us in the headnote, he heard as a child from an elderly relative. The facts of the tale are simple. In the early nineteenth century, Billie Potts keeps a frontier inn in the section of western Kentucky between the Tennessee and Cumberland rivers. He offers hospitality to travelers and then points them down the trail where his accomplice lies in ambush, waiting to rob and murder them. Billie Potts's son, Little Billie, sent to apprise one of his father's accomplices of the approach of an affluent traveler, attempts to kill the man himself only to be beaten to the draw and wounded. Little Billie then quarrels with his parents, journeys to the West, and after ten years returns, wealthy and complacent, to the homestead. Withholding his identity from his parents in order to "tease 'em and fun 'em," Little Billie is brutally murdered by his father who mistakes him for a rich stranger.

The narrative is related in vigorous ballad style, swiftly paced and coarsely comic. But Warren has heavily freighted this fable of the frontier with symbolism and commentary. Interspersed throughout the narrative are parenthetical sections, measured and deliberate, developing the larger implications of the story. This commentary is spoken by a man of the twentieth century who is watching the characters work out their destinies in frontier Kentucky and assessing the meaning of their lives for his own:

> The answer is in the back of the book but the page is gone.
> And grandma told you to tell the truth but she is dead.
> And heedless, their hairy faces fixed
> Beyond your call or question now, they move
> Under the infatuate weight of their wisdom, . . .

The effect is that of juxtaposing past and present, of generalizing the particular facts into an archetypal pattern of the discovery of guilt, the attempt at flight, and the necessity of return: "The long compulsion and the circuit hope/Back." Within the context of the American experience, the pattern is that of the westering pioneer still haunted by the tie to the heartland:

> For Time is always the new place,
> And no-place.
> For Time is always the new name and the new face,
> And no-name and no-face.
>
> For Time is motion
> For Time is innocence
> For Time is West.

There is, however, no more an escape from the past than there is an escape from the self, for the two are indivisible. Like Billie Potts, the modern man must retrace the path that he has followed, even though in seeking the source of his life he may, ironically, find death. He must understand that, in Santayana's famous phrase, the man who cannot remember the past is doomed to repeat it. Man must measure his actions and his dreams against those of all the men who have preceded him:

And you, wanderer, back,
For the beginning is death and the end may be life,
For the beginning was definition and the end may be definition,
For our innocence needs, perhaps, new definition . . .

"A good poem," Warren has said, "is a massive, deep, and vital thing."[13] "The Ballad of Billie Potts" is such a poem, but, despite the inventiveness of its language and the sustained propulsion of its narrative, it does not come off. The mixing of manners, the folk ballad set off against the sophisticated commentary, works to the disadvantage of both by heightening the incongruity. The passages of commentary seem contrived, pretentious in their insistence on wringing profundities from what is, basically, little more than an anecdote, massive in its ironies. By contrast, the ballad seems arch and folksy.

"The Ballad of Billie Potts" does, however, point the direction toward Warren's developing interests. The opening out of the poem, the concern with narrative, suggests that Warren's gift for invention was restive under the limitations of verse and was seeking an outlet in the more ample forms of fiction. Toward the end of the 1930's he returned to the material of his first published fiction, "Prime Leaf," and, with the publication of *Night Rider* in 1939, his career as a novelist was launched.

CHAPTER 3

The Past Recaptured

ROBERT PENN WARREN'S association with the Nashville Fugitives had encouraged him to channel most of his creative energies during the 1920's into the writing of poetry. But after his return from Oxford in 1930 to take a position in the English department at Southwestern College in Memphis, he began more and more to turn his attention to the writing of fiction. "Prime Leaf" had opened a promising vein which he was eager to explore further. Reminiscing about the writing of "Prime Leaf" at Oxford, he recalled "the discovery that you could really enjoy trying to write fiction. It was a new way of looking at things, and my head was full of recollections of the way objects looked in Kentucky and Tennessee. It was like going back to the age of twelve, going fishing and all that. It was a sense of freedom and excitement."[1]

The short stories Warren published during the 1930's are deeply rooted in the Kentucky and Tennessee of his boyhood. "When the Light Gets Green," which appeared in the *Southern Review* in 1936, is closely related in action and atmosphere to "Prime Leaf." The story concerns a small boy's recollection of the death of his grandfather, a gallant old captain of cavalry who had ridden with General Forrest and who had passed his declining years reliving his campaigns with his grandson. The story poignantly conveys the boy's awareness of the pathos of the old man's resignation and of the puzzling emptiness of his own feelings. This youthful narrator is not unlike the shy, baffled high school boy in "Testament of Flood" who discovers that a classmate whom he has secretly pitied and loved is the town harlot. Two stories that appeared in the *Virginia Quarterly Review* during the mid-1930's also exploit Southern themes and settings. "Christmas Gift" delicately traces the growth of human understanding for a share-cropper's son by a town storekeeper and a country doctor. "Her Own People" explores with great subtlety the ambiguous strands of responsibility and guilt that bind a Negro maid and her white employers.[2]

These highly successful efforts at short fiction were only the by-products of a larger ambition—the writing of a novel. From 1931 until 1933 Warren was devoting such hours as he could spare from the classroom to work on "God's Own Time," a novel dealing with life on a Kentucky farm before World War I. Eventually he became dissatisfied with it and began a second which was concerned with a small-town school, but it too has never been published.[3] Then, in 1936, Warren returned to a familiar story of his youth, the uprising of tobacco farmers in Kentucky and Tennessee. To combat the tobacco trusts, the growers had formed the "Dark Tobacco District Planters' Protective Association of Kentucky and Tennessee." The first rally, in which five thousand growers took part, was called at Warren's hometown, Guthrie, Kentucky, during the autumn of 1904. When the corporations attempted to break the Association by paying high prices to the farmers who did not join, the planters formed bands of "night riders" under the leadership of Dr. David A. Amoss and took the law into their own hands. The ensuing violence was climaxed by the dynamiting of company warehouses in Hopkinsville, Kentucky. Dr. Amoss was tried for the murder of a man shot from ambush during the escape, but was not convicted.[4] Warren employed these facts as the framework of his first novel, *Night Rider,* which appeared in 1939.

I

With his sure instinct for the storyteller's art, Warren begins *Night Rider* with one of the most effective means for opening a tale—a traveler on a journey. The novel's central character,

Percy Munn, is wedged into the aisle of a train packed with farmers on the way to Bardsville, Kentucky, to attend a rally of an association of tobacco growers. Alone and aloof, he counters all overtures of human affection with a cold gesture of civility. The other passengers, swept to the same destination, have merged their identity into a shouting crowd which operates as a dehumanizing force, reducing them all to the mindless and all-enveloping surge of a natural catastrophe—a landslip. Percy Munn feels that his own identity is threatened by the physical presence of the crowd. He is disgusted by the "hot weight of flesh" which presses against him as the train slows for the station, and he regrets his decision to leave the seclusion of his remote tobacco farm for the spurious excitements of Bardsville. For the multitudinous human pressures of his life, he is not "braced right." Thus in the opening paragraphs of the novel, the broad outlines of Munn's character are sketched in: his indecisiveness, his sense of helplessness, and his Prufrockian revulsion from, coupled with his perverse attraction to, the coarse earthiness of life.

The plot of *Night Rider* follows with the simplicity of Greek tragedy the descending curve of Percy Munn's destruction. His life is divided between his tobacco farm, which he thinks of as "home," and his law office in Bardsville. Although only mildly interested in the formation of the Association of Growers of Dark Fired Tobacco, Munn is induced by the gruff and assertive planter Bill Christian to attend the organization meeting and then is persuaded to sit on the platform at the rally where the farmers are addressed by Senator Tolliver, a stereotyped version of the silver-tongued politician. Without warning, Munn is called out to speak. Forced to improvise, he speaks movingly of the aims of the Association and is persuaded to the cause by the eloquence of his own rhetoric.

These powers of persuasion make Percy Munn the natural choice to proselytize for the Association among the tobacco growers, but his efforts are thwarted by small planters, rugged and stiff-necked hill folk, who doggedly refuse to sign over their crops to a board of directors. When Senator Tolliver betrays the Association to the tobacco monopoly, Munn joins with Doctor MacDonald and his father-in-law, Professor Ball, in the formation of the Free Farmers' Brotherhood of Protection and Control. This euphemistic title masks a band of night riders whose tactics, reminiscent of the Ku Klux Klan, force reluctant planters into the Association by destroying their crops. When even this fails, the night riders, as a last resort, blow up the warehouses of the tobacco trust.

Infected by the general moral collapse of the community, Munn is driven to murder Bunk Trevelyan, a man whose life he had once saved in court. Trevelyan had pleaded innocent to the knife murder of a neighbor whom he was known to hate and whom he had been heard to threaten. Although Trevelyan is a sullen, slovenly dirt farmer, Munn is drawn to him by his uncomplicated mind and by his readiness to act without regard to consequences. Telling himself he is motivated by an abstract desire for justice, Munn illegally searches some Negro shanties, finds a knife thought to be the murder weapon, and gains a conviction against an old Negro. Trevelyan is then induced to join the night riders but attempts to backmail a member of the band by threatening to inform. Munn urges Trevelyan to flee and, when he refuses, murders him, justifying the act by reasoning that Trevelyan should have been punished for killing his neighbor.

As the night-rider movement crumbles, Doctor MacDonald is arrested on the evidence of an informer, Al Turpin, and is charged with arson and conspiracy. On the day of the trial, Al Turpin is killed as he walks across the courthouse square by a shot fired by Professor Ball from Percy Munn's office window. Munn, charged with the crime, escapes to the hill farm of Willie Proudfit.

The disintegration of Munn's public life is paralleled by the collapse of his private life. His wife, May, is a bland and ineffectual woman whom Munn appears to have courted for some obscure wish to "explain himself to himself." The relationship is without either meaning or affection. The night he murders Trevelyan, Munn returns home and brutally assaults May. She leaves him, and he turns to an affair with Bill Christian's daughter, Lucille. But Lucille too is incapable of love and the affair ends, as did the marriage, in a loveless copulation.

Lucille Christian comes to Willie Proudfit's farm where Munn is in hiding to tell him of her father's death and to ask him to marry her. Willie learns from his bigoted and mean-spirited nephew, Sylvestus, that Lucille had come to Munn's room during the night. Rebuked by Willie, Munn leaves the farm motivated by a final expiatory act—killing Senator Tolliver, who now seems the sum of all villainy. Incapable of the deed, Munn is shot down as he flees Tolliver's house. Sylvestus had informed. Ironically, Munn is innocent of the particular acts for which he dies. Sylvestus was mistaken in believing that Munn had committed adultery with Lucille at Willie's house, yet Munn is an adulterer. Similarly, Munn is not guilty of the murder of Al Turpin for which the posse kills him, yet Munn is a murderer.

Such a summary of the plot, while it calls attention to the directness of the narrative line and the skillful handling of the irony, fails to do justice to the thematic richness of *Night Rider*. Percy Munn is the prototype of the most familiar of all Warren characters. He is a man obsessed with the need to know himself, to plumb the "darkly coiling depth within himself" (162). He longs for self-definition, for what he called the "unifying fulfillment" (208). His actions spring from his awareness that he is a divided man and from his longing for identity, for integration of self. His life resembles the stereopticon of his childhood. Gazing through the lenses, he had seen a "rich, three-dimensional little world. . . . He had felt that if he could just break through into that little world . . . he would know the most unutterable bliss." He cannot, however, superimpose the fragmented elements of his nature. His life is without depth and substance, like the stereopticon cards held in his hand, "the flat, dull, fading picture printed in duplicate" (161).

The sense of alienation is heavy upon him. He seizes desperately upon a warm human gesture, a sympathetic face in a crowd or a word of appreciation, for he longs to understand fully another human being and hence himself. When he hears the speech and song of men partaking warmly and generously of their common humanity, he is torn between his sudden heightened awareness of human brotherhood and his sense of deprivation at being powerless to share it.

Percy Munn's numbed sensibilities are equaled by his paralysis of the will. He longs to realize himself in action, but he is unwittingly shaped by the stronger wills about him. Invited to join the board of directors of the Association, he instinctively blurts out "no!"—but he joins. Asked to scrape plant beds with the night riders, he replies: "It just isn't in me, I reckon"—but he scrapes them. When he is confronted with an account in the newspapers of events in which he was involved, he feels "as if he were reading of something in which he had had no part" (173). When he does act, it is action disengaged from thought as when he impulsively punches a man who jokingly implied that Munn had rigged a jury.

The duality of Munn's nature is dramatized in *Night Rider* by Warren's handling of the imagery of darkness and light. Night and day reveal the two aspects of Munn's character which are ultimately irreconcilable: "He thought how the night may be, in truth, mirror to the day, returning the reflection of a man's self to him twisted and confused and almost unrecognizable like the reflection in a flawed, pocked, and dirty glass, or in those contorting mirrors you see in tent shows, or in disturbed water" (177). The opening scenes of the novel are bathed in blazing sunlight, but Percy Munn, a man "locked inside the darkness that [is] himself," instinctively seeks out the shadows (177). He prefers the darkened privacy of his hotel room in Bardsville, the cool gloom of the stables, and the dim obscurity of the tobacco barns. Early in the novel he marvels that "night changed everything, even the most accustomed landscape, your own fields. Or the face of somebody you knew and loved" (149). He secretly studies the face of his wife in sleep, hoping to find something that will explain either her or, by reflection, himself.

Munn seems most at ease by night, for the bright blue vault of the sky stirs uneasy speculations in him. It is a vast emptiness and hollowness under which he finds no comfort or serenity.

At the end of the first day of proselytizing for the Association, he finds solace in the "comfort of the night and isolation" (41). As his involvement with the Association increases, his mind seems like an "eye unseeing but straining forward into the dark" (46). Munn's first illegal action, the shakedown of the Negro cabins, takes place under the "uneven light of the moon," and a deepening darkness closes over the novel as it moves toward its conclusion.

The pivotal scene of *Night Rider* is the one in which Munn takes the oath of the Brotherhood for Protection and Control. To join the night riders, Munn must ride to an abandoned sawmill deep in the woods. In the "dark shadow" that envelops the mill, men stand alone, mute, suspicious, their faces only a "whitish blur." When Munn hears his name called to summon him to the mill, he is startled at the strangeness of the sound of the familiar word. He enters the "blacker, interior darkness" of the mill, gropes unseeingly down a black corridor, only to be thrust suddenly into a room brilliantly illuminated by the beam from a reflector lantern. Physically blinded by the glare, the equivalent of the moral blindness of the act he will perform, Munn takes the oath.

> "Come forward," the voice said, and he walked across the intervening ten feet or so of floor toward the lantern and the voice. He passed beyond the range of the lantern's rays, was completely blind for an instant before his eyes could accustom themselves to the dark, and then saw the man standing behind the table that supported the lantern, and the other men sitting on benches and boxes beyond.
>
> (156)

Munn's decision to embark on a career of violence and lawlessness is the central and irrevocable action of his life—from this act all else follows. The significance of the action is heightened and focused by the movement from light to darkness, the dominant pattern of imagery of the novel.

As Munn's despair deepens, his actions seem to him like the "blows of a blind man who strikes out at the undefined sounds which penetrate his private darkness." His mind grazes off tangentially from the issue at hand to a "confused darkness of speculation." With the ultimate violence, the dynamiting of the company warehouses, Munn believes "it will all be. different. It will all be clear as day." But this too fails, and eventually he becomes a creature of the night, cowering like an animal in his cave, afraid to venture into the light. The final scene of the novel, the final sentence, reinforces and resolves this night symbolism. Stumbling with plunging strides, Munn runs for the "woods, the absorbing darkness." Shot down, he hears, "so empty in the darkness," the shouts of his pursuers, "like the voices of boys at a game in the dark."

Warren's development of the two women in Percy Munn's life, his wife, May, and his mistress, Lucille Christian, further emphasizes both the symbolic pattern of darkness and light and the deep-seated division of self. Whereas he sees May generally in brilliant sunshine in her garden or in a meadow, he knows Lucille only in the dark. When she comes to him for the last time, Lucille recalls the fact to him: "You know, we've never talked, not really talked, you and me, in the light" (435). Munn first sees Lucille standing "in complete stillness, in absorbed repose," and he, mistaking the appearance for the reality, hopes to find in her the serenity of spirit for which he longs. She stimulates his "appetite for definition, for certainty" (251). Yet Lucille has sought the same thing in Percy Munn, for she too has a divided nature:

> She was, it seemed to him, two persons. There was the person who came to his room, and stood with one finger to her lips while she gently pushed the shadowy white door shut behind her; and there was the person whom he saw moving about the house in the daytime, talking casually and easily to him or her father . . . The two persons seemed quite distinct to him.
>
> (240-41)

Lucille also longs for the unifying fulfillment. She tells Munn, echoing his own words earlier in the novel, "If everything, everything you were and wanted and owed to people—everything—matched up just once, even for just a minute so you were really one person, completely, then you would be almost too happy to live" (241).

Among the characters in *Night Rider*, only the enigmatic Captain Todd seems to possess the "inner certainty of self" (43) for which Percy Munn and Lucille Christian hunger. Captain Todd has about him the air of conviction and confidence which Munn attributes to his life of action. Todd had heroically fought the Yankees during the Civil War, and after Appomattox he had captured and summarily hanged the bushwhackers and guerrillas who preyed on a defeated and demoralized South. But whatever the source of the Captain's "ripe, secret security," it remains hidden behind a mask of amiable gravity.

The possibility of fulfillment in action which Munn finds so compelling in the life of Captain Todd also attracts him to Willie Proudfit, the farmer at whose home he hides after his escape from Bardsville. In the closing pages of the novel, Willie tells his story, a *tour de force* of dialect narrative at which Warren excels. Proudfit had traveled West, alone, killing buffalo and fighting Indians. He had wrested from the wilderness a confidence in self which he cannot articulate but which he manifests in the actions of his life. Like Captain Todd, Proudfit has won from the past a meaning, and he recounts his life with modesty but with a consciousness of its significance.

The contrast with Percy Munn's life is extreme. Munn had traveled East to study law and to spend his afternoons reading fragmentary and irrelevant items from the newspapers to an elderly and eccentric cousin, Miss Ianthe Sprague. She has no memory of the past nor any desire to remember it, "for out of memory rises the notion of a positive and purposive future, the revision of the past" (212). Integration of self is dependent on a sense of continuity with the past and faith in the future. But Munn, like Miss Sprague, must "protect himself by denying memory, as it were, from the contact of the self he had been. And his mind closed like a valve against all thoughts of the future" (219). The lesson Willie Proudfit learned from the past, salvation through righteousness, makes no impression on Munn.

Quite the contrary, he leaves the farm for a final act of vengeance, the murder of Senator Tolliver.

Related to Munn's failure to grasp the meaning of the past for the present is his besetting sin of abstraction. For Munn the Association becomes the idea incarnate, a means to salvation beyond the flux of history. His first speech to the farmers dramatizes the force of the idea: "There is nothing here but an idea" (26). And later, "The Association, that was what he was now, if he was anything." He feels at last that his allegiance to the idea and his thirst for action will be realized in a single moment of truth, the dynamiting of the company warehouses— "that reeling moment of certainty and fulfillment." But even the immaculate idea is at the mercy of human inadequacy. At the trial of Doctor MacDonald the act of violence is analyzed and dissected, and the Truth becomes not a thing indivisible, but the multiple truths of the many fallible human beings who are involved: "The truths of those people were not the truth that had been his that night; but truth was his no longer. The truth: it devoured and blotted out each particular truth, each individual man's truth, it crushed truths as under a blundering tread, it was blind" (365).

Night Rider is a remarkably mature and polished first novel. In it Warren has created a complete fictional world, a world of substance and texture which is peculiarly coherent and self-contained. Warren's delight in action and suspense, his variety and depth of characterization, and his exuberant and imaginative use of language are already clearly apparent. Also, there is manifest in this first novel the same feeling for form, the insistence on design, which characterizes his poetry. Like Thomas Hardy and Joseph Conrad, novelists to whom he had obviously apprenticed himself, Warren has a firm grasp of the architectonics of his craft.

The question of form is crucial to the success of *Night Rider,* for, in choosing Percy Munn for his center of consciousness, Warren was taking a calculated risk. In telling the story from the point of view of a befuddled and divided character, he might have blurred his effects and left the meaning of his work ultimately obscure. But Warren is too sophisticated a critic not to have been aware of the problem. In 1935 in an essay on Thomas Wolfe, Warren complained that *Of Time and the River* had no organizing principle, no clearly delineated character at the center of the novel to give the raw materials of Wolfe's personal experience design and direction:[5]

> It may be objected [Warren wrote] that other works of literary art, and very great ones at that, have heroes who defy definition and who are merely centers of "fury." For instance, there is Hamlet or Lear. But a difference may be observed. Those characters may defy the attempt at central definition, but the play hangs together in each case as a structure without such definition; that is, there has been no confusion between the sensibility that produced the play as an object of art, and the sensibility of a hero in a play.

No such confusion is evident in *Night Rider*. In fact, Warren's detachment from his hero is clearly evident, notably in his habit of referring to him throughout the novel as *Mr.* Munn. Because Munn does defy central definition, his remoteness from the reader is the significant thing about him. He is equally remote from himself and from his world—he is one of the hollow men. But since we see the story from his point of view, we must infer this hollowness from the complex of situations and relationships which constitutes the structure of the novel. The effect is difficult to achieve, and Warren may have felt that he was only partially successful; for in his second novel, *At Heaven's Gate*, he experimented with a more varied handling of the angle of vision than that employed in *Night Rider*.

II

"*Night Rider*," Robert Penn Warren told an interviewer in 1957, "is the world of my youth. *At Heaven's Gate* is contemporary."[6] Upon its publication in 1943, *At Heaven's Gate* prompted a certain amount of speculation concerning its sources in Warren's experience. Malcolm Cowley professed to see in the city which is the locus of the novel a thinly disguised Nashville, Tennessee, "with a few traits borrowed from Memphis." The university, he thought, might be Vanderbilt and the group of intellectuals the Fugitives. As for the finance capitalist at the center of the novel, Bogan Murdock, Cowley found him reminiscent of Colonel Luke Lee, a former United States Senator and securities manipulator who went to jail for his part in the collapse of a Nashville bank.[7]

But to label *At Heaven's Gate* a *roman à clef* would be to undervalue a powerful and intricately wrought work of art. It is a long and brutal novel, forceful in style and filled with scenes freshly observed and vividly rendered. Warren himself has given us a clue to the importance he attributes to his conception. It was Dante's Seventh Circle, he tells us, "that provided, with some liberties of interpretation and extension, the basic scheme and metaphor for the whole novel. All of the main characters are violators of nature." The businessman hero, Bogan Murdock, "was supposed to embody, in one of his dimensions, the desiccating abstraction of power, to be a violator of nature, a usurer of Dante's Seventh Circle, and to try to fulfill vicariously his natural emptiness by exercising power over those around him."[8]

The house of Murdock is, like Faulkner's Sartoris clan, a family in decline. Bogan Murdock can trace his ancestry to Andrew Jackson, and a portrait of the Old Hero hangs on the wall in the Murdock library. Bogan's father, Major Lemuel Murdock, "fought four bitter years for the defense and honor of his native state" (133). Then, in defense of his own "honor," he murdered his opponent in a gubernatorial election for charging, accurately, that Murdock had worked hand in glove with carpetbaggers. Bogan himself has risen to wealth and influence through the manipulation of securities which, he admits in a moment of crisis, is "decidedly illegal" (344). Bogan's wife, Dorothy, boasts a great-great-grandfather who was a general in the American Revolution and a grandfather who was a Senator in the Confederate Congress. Her father, however, died a failure;

and Dorothy is, as her husband sums her up, a "drunken, sodden, self-abusing, middle-aged bitch" (347).

Bogan Murdock has created a world by the sheer force of superior personality, a "special type of subtle pressure" (249). He uses politeness as other men use force; as his daughter, Sue, says, "It's just a way of making people do things" (6). Murdock's gift is a cold detachment from and an understanding of the ways of men. He analyzes college football with the same passionless objectivity he employs in his business deals, and his justification of professionalism in collegiate athletics is the same as his rationale for the juggling of stocks and bonds: ". . . since we do not enjoy the satisfaction of virtue, we might at least enjoy the satisfaction of efficiency" (20). He can discover no irony in justifying his own conduct by quoting the Emperor Tiberius. The reader never enters the consciousness of Bogan Murdock. He is seen from several discrete points of view, but chiefly through the eyes of two people who fall fatally under his spell: Jerry Calhoun, who willingly and gratefully comes under his influence and is destroyed by it, and Murdock's daughter, Sue, who is destroyed by her efforts to rebel from it.

When he first enters the world of Bogan Murdock, Jerry Calhoun appears to be a "kindly, awkward, humble monster." Sue Murdock, coming upon him in her father's living room, wonders "where in the world he had come from" (40). The world out of which Jerry came is certainly the opposite of Sue Murdock's world. His mother died at his birth, and his father is a clumsy, inept dirt farmer whom his son considers a failure. His Uncle Lew, a waspish and clubfooted misanthrope, seems to Jerry like the images the old man carves from peach stones, "not animal and not quite human" (45). His great-aunt Ursula sits blind and dirty in a corner rocker, waited on by an aged and incompetent Negro housekeeper. Jerry's youth seems to him, in retrospect, "ugly, monotonous, fumbling, and dirty" (52).

Jerry's prowess as an All-American at the University calls him to the attention of Bogan Murdock, whose world represents to Jerry an escape from the ugliness and poverty of his youth.

Murdock's corruption of Jerry is subtly conceived. He joins a fraternity allowing an "anonymous alumnus" to pay his initiation fee. Offered a job selling bonds in Murdock's firm, Jerry instantly rejects a graduate fellowship at the university. Murdock himself adds the finishing touches: trips to New York to rub off the provincial edges, invitations to ride to hounds, the address of the right tailor, election to the right clubs.

At Murdock's suggestion, Jerry submits himself to the tutorials of an eccentric economist, Duckfoot Blake. Blake's advice on the methods of selling bonds, given ironically, is accepted humorlessly by Jerry as gospel. Blake's home where they frequently work is sufficiently reminiscent of Jerry's own home to fill him with "discomfort and revulsion" (79). Yet there is a part of him which clings nostalgically to the memories of his earlier life which, in comparison with his present sophistication, seems uncomplicated and uncluttered.

Jerry's divided attitude toward Blake's home and his own is but the symptom of a deeper division within himself. "It was," he thinks, "like there were two Jerry Calhouns, the Jerry Calhoun to whom it had happened and the Jerry Calhoun to whom nothing had happened" (232). He finds himself baffled and lost in the "vast conspiracy" of the world (31). He achieves the goal which all of "Murdock's boys" long for, engagement to the "Infanta," Sue Murdock, and is later rejected by her as an inferior version, if not an agent, of her father. At such moments of crisis, he can only repeat his name like some talismanic device which may evoke the reality which is himself: "Jerry Calhoun, who was Jerry Calhoun, who was Jerry—" (34).

Sue Murdock dismisses Jerry because she understands his weakness but not her own. "Oh, you'll die rich," she tells him, but "you're an emotional cripple" (99). Sue, too, is emotionally crippled, for she has little knowledge of what she is or of what she wants. A beautiful, spoiled woman, she offers no defense for her conduct beyond an insistence on her immediate desires. When her brother inquires why she jilted Jerry, she answers, "Because I wanted to" (209). When Slim Sarrett, a student at the university, suggests she become a writer, she replies, "I don't want to be." When Sarrett attempts to analyze the "special complex of forces represented by the word *want*," Sue is not interested (147). For her "it's a damned good reason" (209). She acts, as Jerry observes, "like the minute was all there was, like there wasn't any yesterday and there wasn't any tomorrow, or like what yesterday was or tomorrow would be didn't have any connection" (117). Fitfully interested in the theater, Sue feels most alive when impersonating another. After leaving Jerry, she feels like an actress rehearsing a part, "beautiful and empty like a dream" (152). "Oh, what am I?" she asks, and her cry is echoed by her mother's "I don't know what I am" (185).

Sue's life is a cycle of things desperately desired and, once obtained, just as desperately despised: a Northern finishing school, her debut, Jerry Calhoun, escape from her father. It is this last which drives her to impetuous and spectacular extremes of conduct. Unlike Jerry Calhoun, who only spasmodically and dimly grasps the fact that he hates his father because he wishes to be free of the past which the older man represents, Sue quite frankly despises her father and violently rejects him. Of her father she says: "Because he made me he thinks he owns me." Her cry epitomizes the plight of all who populate Bogan Murdock's world, for he did make them what they are and he exacts an unswerving allegiance.

Both Jerry and Sue come to grief in their efforts to cope with the world of Bogan Murdock. Jerry ends in jail as the scapegoat in the collapse of Murdock's financial empire. Sue drifts restlessly from man to man, finding in each some haunting resemblance to her hated father. After breaking her engagement to Jerry, she becomes the mistress of Slim Sarrett, a graduate student, boxer, and poet. She leaves him and enters into a sordid liaison with Jason Sweetwater, a union official dedicated to breaking the power of Bogan Murdock. Pregnant with Sweetwater's child, Sue undergoes an abortion; and, while recovering in her apartment, she is strangled by the crazed Sarrett.

Earlier in the novel Sarrett, in the presence of Sue, had exposed Murdock's fundamental flaw: "You . . . represent to me the special disease of our time, the abstract passion for power, a vanity springing from an awareness of the emptiness and unreality of the self which can only attempt to become real and human by the oppression of people who manage to retain some shreds of reality and humanity" (250). Slim Sarrett understands the motives of Bogan Murdock for he shares them—his passion for power is equally insatiable. In the dialogue between Slim and Sue which opens the novel, Slim can see no reason for riding a horse. It is too easy to master a brute beast; "the true contest should be to set oneself against another human being" (4).

Like Bogan Murdock, Slim has created a world by the magnetism of his own personality, a world which is centered in his studio-apartment. He prepares the introduction of each new person "as scrupulously and as cunningly as a dramatist prepares the entrance of a hero" (204). For Slim art, not finance, is the central reality. He speaks grandly of his role, for he is pretentiously, self-consciously the *artist*. "An artist, a poet, never feels the need to 'make up' anything. . . . He finds in facts ample occupation, and he can afford to face them. . . . The artist is the enemy of blur" (150). Yet his art is as desiccated, abstract, and sterile in its own way as Murdock's finance. To men like Duckfoot Blake, it is a "conspiracy among introverts . . . and intellectual tat-and-crochet boys" (203). And despite Slim's insistence that the artist does not need to "make up" anything, his own life is an enormous lie. His world collapses when, at the height of a party at his studio, Billie Constantidopeles, an old friend, appears unexpectedly to reveal that Slim's father was not a riverboat captain blown up under picturesque circumstances but a vacuum cleaner salesman from Georgia and that Slim is a homosexual.

Slim's sickness, like Jerry Calhoun's, is a disruption of sensibility. But unlike Jerry, Slim cultivates and savors the duality of his nature. He boasts of leading a "double life which every artist is forced by his nature to lead" (165). Vain of his reputation as both college boxer and poet, he makes no effort to integrate his several roles: "I happen to prefer to keep my special physical discipline disjunct from my esthetic discipline—from my poetry"

(102). This inner division is further emphasized by Slim's sexual ambivalence.

Slim has a compulsive, voyeuristic obsession to analyze other people, for he knows that they talk about themselves out of a desire to define themselves. His own poetry is such a dialogue. It is Slim who, in a seminar paper, articulates the quest of all the major characters of the novel—each is groping toward some kind of self-knowledge:

"The tragic flaw in the Shakespearean hero is a defect in self-knowledge. . . . Bacon wrote: Knowledge is power. Bacon was thinking of knowledge of the mechanisms of the external world. Shakespeare wrote: Self-knowledge is power. Shakespeare was thinking of the mechanisms of the spirit, to which the mechanisms of the external world, including other persons, are instruments. In other words, Shakespeare was interested in success. By success, he meant: Self-fulfillment. But his tragedy is concerned with failure. Naturally. The successful man . . . offers only the smooth surface, like an egg. In so far as he is truly successful, he has no story. He is pure. But poetry is concerned only with failure, distortion, imbalance—with impurity. And poetry itself is impurity. The pure cry of pain is not poetry. The pure gasp and sigh of love is not poetry. Poetry is the impurity which an active being secretes to become pure. It is the glitter of pus, richer than Ind, the monument in dung, the oyster's pearl" (196).

The worlds of Bogan Murdock and Slim Sarrett constitute the two worlds of the novel. Together they represent what Jack Burden, the narrator of *All the King's Men,* calls the "terrible division of the age," the dissociation of sensibility which Jack diagnoses as the sickness of contemporary society. Characters who are at home in one world are ill at ease in the other. Slim and Rosemary, a crippled student at the university whom Sue has befriended, are hopelessly out of place when invited to the Murdock estate. Similarly, Jerry and Bogan's son, Hammond, are equally misplaced in Slim's bohemian studio. In a symbolic scene, Bogan Murdock and Slim Sarrett confront one another in Sue's apartment. Forced to choose between them, Sue exchanges one world for another but cannot survive the change. She is outraged by her father's world; she is murdered by Sarrett when she rejects his world.

Two characters in *At Heaven's Gate* move easily between these two worlds and link them together. Both are men whose knowledge of self makes them at home in any world. Jason Sweetwater has made his work his life. "A man could not believe in himself unless he believed in something else"; such is the sum of his wisdom. And Sweetwater understands Slim Sarrett: "He is a liar just like a channel catfish ain't a canary. He swims in a lie, and he is in the lie and the lie is in him. . . . He lives in a dream world" (303-4). And there is Duckfoot Blake, who in his breezy cynicism and wisecracking speech looks forward to Jack Burden in *All the King's Men*. Duckfoot finds the same unreality principle in Bogan Murdock that Sweetwater finds in Slim Sarrett: "Bogan Murdock is just a dream Bogan Murdock had, a great big wonderful dream" (373). Duckfoot, like Sweetwater, has won from adversity a measure of affirmation, the knowledge that "everything he had ever done or said or thought mattered" (372).

Set off against the worlds of Murdock and Sarrett is yet another world of the novel, that of Ashby Wyndham. In intercalary chapters throughout *At Heaven's Gate,* Warren has introduced the "Statement of Ashby Wyndham," a narrative cast in the form of a condemned man's confession. The story, at first apparently unrelated to the main narrative, converges on it slowly but inevitably like the superimposed images of a rangefinder, giving depth and dimension to the themes of the novel. Ashby Porsum Wyndham is a headstrong, semi-literate backwoods farmer. Having sinned against his brother, he undergoes a spiritual conversion when he has a vision of his dead infant son. He starts down the river on a houseboat, stopping at towns to preach the gospel to all who will listen. He and his disciples arrive eventually at the city which is the setting of the novel. Ashby's spiritual pride leads him to destroy, one by one, the lives of those around him. His flaw is a defect in self-knowledge, and his plight is genuinely tragic. He, too, builds a world by the eloquence of his tongue and the force of his will, only to see it collapse as a result of his overweening drive for power over others. His story cuts across the main line of the narrative at a point where his cousin, Private Porsum, a hero of World War I and a Murdock puppet, finds himself fatally compromised by his involvement in Murdock's financial schemes. Reading Ashby's confession, Porsum repents and breaks with Murdock, the act that brings Murdock's empire crashing down.

Like Willie Proudfit of *Night Rider,* Ashby Wyndham has confronted his past and has come to terms with it. In so doing, he stands in marked contrast to most of the other characters of the novel, who, like Percy Munn, deny the past or fail to grasp its meaning. Sue Murdock will not admit the past's claim upon her. Jerry Calhoun has "shut his mind resolutely to any thought of the past" (22), and in a final moment of illumination, he must face the fact that he wanted the people who shared that past—Aunt Ursula, Uncle Lew, even his father—dead. Bogan Murdock and Slim Sarrett repudiate the past by rejecting their real fathers and creating imaginary fathers that satisfy their image of themselves. Jason Sweetwater and Duckfoot Blake stand apart from these characters in their acceptance of the past, symbolized by their acceptance of their fathers.

The evangelical Christianity of Ashby Wyndham and the rather bleak affirmations of Sweetwater and Blake are the only positive notes of a novel in which the pervasive tone is nihilistic. The act of love is either blindly compulsive or coldly analytic. "I don't love anybody," Sue cries, and her words are echoed by her mother's "I don't love anything." Images of decay and disease, reminiscent of Warren's use of motifs from *The Waste Land* in his early poetry, dominate the novel. There is the unremitting commentary of Uncle Lew who speaks of Lemuel Murdock as a "murdering blackguard swole with pride pus." Jason Sweetwater observes that a man has got "to boil the pus out." Slim Sarrett is concerned with the "dung and offal" which fertilize his art.

Warren's use of Eliotic imagery calls attention to the various literary influences to which he was responding and which are reflected in *At Heaven's Gate.* In speaking of his first two novels, Warren has said that "there was a good deal of the shadow not only of the events of that period but of the fiction of that period."[9] But influence hunting, a game fraught with the danger of mistaking the shadow for the substance, is especially perilous in the case of Warren. Few writers of our time have been more sensitive to the shaping power of the literary tradition and perhaps none has read more widely and deeply.

At Heaven's Gate, set as it is in the 1920's, inevitably invites comparison with the novels which have shaped our picture of that decade. Warren has said that the young people about whom F. Scott Fitzgerald wrote "were groping to find some satisfaction in a world from which the old values had been withdrawn."[10] The same could be said of the young people of *At Heaven's Gate.* Jerry Calhoun is a blood brother to the "bond man," Nick Carraway, in *The Great Gatsby,* and Sue Murdock is reminiscent of Daisy Buchanan in the same novel or, for that matter, any of a number of Fitzgerald heroines, the beautiful and damned. Fitzgerald had employed in *Gatsby* a kind of dual hero: Nick Carraway and Jay Gatsby, the one a cautious skeptic and the other an exuberant dreamer. Together they constitute two aspects of a single American character. This technique is analogous to Warren's paralleling of Slim Sarrett and Jerry Calhoun. And in *Tender Is the Night* Fitzgerald had anticipated Warren in his analysis of what Willard Thorp has called "the vampirism of the rich,"[11] their need to drain the talent and vitality of their economic inferiors. The tone of post-war disenchantment that pervades Fitzgerald's fiction, the pathos of mangled and dislocated lives, Warren also found in his reading of Ernest Hemingway, notably in *The Sun Also Rises.* Warren learned from Hemingway how to express compassion without stating it baldly. And occasionally the staccato, understated Hemingway manner insinuates itself into the dialogue of *At Heaven's Gate.*

It is, however, Warren's fellow Southerner William Faulkner whom he most closely resembles in both manner and matter. Warren, we know, followed Faulkner's career closely and admiringly—his essay in appreciation is the most penetrating critique of Faulkner's work that we have.[12] Their fiction has much in common: the lush rhetoric, the brooding meditations on the past, the exploitation of the traditional order for its symbolic value in the present. In philosophical weight and tragic intensity Faulkner goes beyond Warren, just as he goes beyond all other American writers of this century, but Warren has created a broader range of characters than Faulkner and is considerably superior in his handling of urbane, sophisticated people. And Warren's knowledge of the variety of contemporary life, particularly his knowledge of regions outside the South, has given his work a broader scope than Faulkner allowed himself.

More profitable than searching for point-by-point influences in Warren's fiction is seeing his work against the two dominant literary tendencies of the time—Naturalism and Symbolism. For a definition of Naturalism we can turn to Warren himself, who defined it in the course of a discussion of T. S. Stribling:[13] "The naturalist novelist took science as the source of his method and his philosophy. His method was, professedly, objective and transcriptive; he was concerned with fact, not value. Motivation of human conduct was to be understood in terms of biology, biochemistry and such."

It would do violence to Warren's fiction to try to force it into such a strait jacket as this, but both *Night Rider* and *At Heaven's Gate* exhibit much of Naturalistic theory and method. Both are big books filled with panoramic scenes pulsing with vitality. In *Night Rider* Warren utilizes the characteristic milieu of the Naturalistic novel in which man becomes a hunted and tortured animal. In *At Heaven's Gate* atavistic impulses lurk just below the thin veneer of civilized behavior. The attention to social class, ranging in *At Heaven's Gate* from financier to dirt farmer, suggests the slice-of-life so admired by the early Naturalists. An amply documented picture of society is occasionally described in a scientific terminology drawn particularly from chemistry and physiology. In both novels the central characters find themselves in the familiar Naturalistic predicament: the individual submerged by social forces which he only dimly understands and which he is powerless to control. These Naturalistic elements in Warren's first two novels link them to a distinguished American tradition which includes the work of Frank Norris, Theodore Dreiser, and Sherwood Anderson.

With certain tendencies of the Naturalists, however, Warren is clearly out of sympathy, notably with their notorious hostility to form stemming from their belief that, since life is patternless, a plot must be a violation of truth. Warren's characters are molded by their pasts, but he never succumbs to a simplistic reliance on heredity and environment to explain human conduct. Certainly the materialism of the Naturalists, what Warren has called the "vision of the God-abandoned and sanction-stripped world of natural process,"[14] had little imaginative appeal for him.

Developing parallel to Naturalism was Symbolism, a tradition widely at variance with Naturalism in its aims and methods. Opposed to the Naturalist's tendency to adopt a mechanistic view of nature and a social conception of man is the Symbolist's tendency to stress an organic view of nature and the individuality of man. The Naturalist turns outward to the external world to observe life with objectivity and to record it in the impersonal language of science. The Symbolist turns inward on his own ego to savor what in his nature is idiosyncratic. He consequently finds himself troubled with a problem of communication. Since his feelings and emotions are unique, he must invent a new language to convey his uniqueness. Although such a language will necessarily be private and difficult, working more by suggestion and intimation than by direct expression, this very imprecision may be a source of strength. The Symbolic novel has an aura of uncertainty which, paradoxically, may charge the work with a vibrant sense of reality. It has an extra dimension, an imaginative margin of ambiguity which adds emotional resonance and artistic power. Warren seems to have had some such idea in mind when he spoke of "that feeling of a mysterious depth which is one of the chief beauties of the art"[15] of fiction. His use of the richly suggestive symbolism of light and dark in *Night Rider* and of disease and decay in *At Heaven's Gate* gives these works a heightened meaning that is unavailable to the doctrinaire naturalist.

Edmund Wilson has said that "the literary history of our time is to a great extent that of the development of Symbolism and of its fusion or conflict with Naturalism."[16] In *Night Rider* and *At Heaven's Gate* Warren demonstrates how both of these traditions might be exploited. In his third novel, *All the King's Men*, he fuses them powerfully and imaginatively, the one reinforcing the other; and the result is one of the great novels of American literature.

CHAPTER 4

The Past and Its Burden

THE IDEA for the work which eventually developed into *All the King's Men* came to Robert Penn Warren during the winter of 1937-38 while he was teaching at Louisiana State University. As his starkly prophetic poems of that period "Ransom" and "Letter from a Coward to a Hero" reveal, Warren was meditating on the principles of decency and democracy and their capacity to survive in the face of deepening economic crisis at home and rampant nationalism abroad. The time seemed to him, as he said later, "a period of unmasking of blank power."[1] His conception for the projected work centered on a dictatorial Southern politician whose motives, though prompted by idealism, are corrupted by the abuse of power. Warren was drawn to the paradox of the politician whose well-spring of power is his ability to satisfy vicariously the needs of the people he governs but whose exercise of that power leads him to the discovery of his moral hollowness. Senator Tolliver of *Night Rider,* sucking vitality from the anonymous crowds he addresses, is a preliminary sketch for such a figure.

Warren first planned a verse play, and the original version entitled "Proud Flesh" was written chiefly in Rome in 1939.[2] But he was dissatisfied with the work in dramatic form, and abandoned it as he became increasingly absorbed in *At Heaven's Gate.* The two works are, however, related thematically. In a preface to *All the King's Men* written in 1953, Warren said that the novel was "a continuation of the experience of writing *At Heaven's Gate,* just as that novel had been, in a way, a continuation of *Proud Flesh.*"[3] This thematic continuity is in part owing to Warren's habit of keeping several works in progress simultaneously. "I generally carry several novels around in me," he told Harvey Breit. "I have to carry things around for so long that they're all overlapping."[4]

When *All the King's Men* appeared in 1946, the reviewers seized immediately upon its resemblance to Huey P. Long and his political regime in Louisiana. Long was the dominant figure in Southern politics while Warren was teaching at Memphis and Nashville during the early 1930's, and after moving to Louisiana State University in 1934, he had an opportunity to observe the results of Longism at first hand. But just as the intervening years have made the novel's debt to the Long legend seem the least important thing about it, so the importance of Long himself has dwindled in the perspective of history. The shenanigans of the Louisiana Kingfish seem less ominous than they once did. It is difficult now to re-create the mood of depression-era Louisiana when the young Hodding Carter, now editor of the Greenville Delta *Democrat-Times,* lay by a roadside armed with a shotgun, waiting to open fire on Huey Long's state troopers, a personal army known as "Huey's Cossacks."[5] The Southern dictator who travestied democratic processes has been metamorphosed into a folk figure, part comic bumpkin and part homespun philosopher after the manner of a Southern Will Rogers.

The biblical allusions in Huey Long's speeches not only gave an evangelical quality to his drive for power but also testified to his devout training in a Baptist home in the piny woods region of north-central Louisiana. Long married at nineteen, worked as a traveling salesman to support himself and his wife, and, incredibly, completed a three-year law course at Tulane Law School in eight months. By turns cunning and candid, belligerent and vindictive, he systematically and skillfully built a monolithic political machine which placed him in the Louisiana governor's chair by the time he was thirty-five. With a growing squad of bodyguards hovering in the background, he survived physical assaults, political attacks, and impeachment proceedings until, when the voters sent him to the United States Senate in 1932, he was the undisputed dictator of Louisiana.

Typed in his day as a fascist or an ignorant buffoon, Huey Long was actually a complex man of remarkable intellectual gifts who defies easy classification. Many of his neighbors loved him and reverently recalled the accomplishments of his administration: a splendid network of highways, elimination of the poll tax, expansion of hospital services, and generous appropriations for the public schools. The claims are indisputable. Yet they were realized by an administration which was a cheerful combination of pragmatism and cynicism, persuasion and coercion. The moralists groaned, but the roads were built. "We got the roads in Louisiana," Long said. "In some states they only have the graft."[6]

Long was in his time, and is today, an enigma. Nowhere were the contradictory elements in his character more clearly manifested than in his relations with Louisiana State University. When Warren arrived there in 1934, he found abundant evidence of Long's achievement and his high-handed tactics. "This is," Long liked to say, "my university."[7] He poured money into classrooms and dormitories, including the million-dollar Huey P. Long Field House. The enrollment doubled, then doubled again. When the school newspaper dared to criticize him, he suspended it. When Warren and his colleagues founded the *Southern Review* in 1935, the possibility of interference caused them to agree to resign if their editorial prerogatives were challenged. They were not, however, subjected to either political or academic pressure during their tenure as editors.[8]

Huey Long was assassinated in the Capitol at Baton Rouge on September 8, 1935, by Dr. Carl Austin Weiss, Jr. Weiss's motives were apparently more personal than political. His father, while head of the state medical association, had fought Long's meddling in faculty affairs of the medical school of Tulane University. Weiss's father-in-law, a state judge, was about to be gerrymandered out of his office, and Long had implied that there was Negro blood in the judge's family. Long's death, like so much else in his career, was melodramatic, and his story has ever since had a magnetic appeal for novelists. Hamilton Basso, in *Sun in Capricorn*, treated the theme superficially and inconclusively. John Dos Passos' *Number One* is indebted to the Long story as is Sinclair Lewis' *It Can't Happen Here*. In 1946, the same year as *All the King's Men*, Adria Locke Langley published *A Lion Is in the Street*. Readers of these novels who remember Huey Long will probably agree with Louis D. Rubin, Jr., that it is *All the King's Men* "that best captures the picture of the historical Kingfish, and of Louisiana in the 1920's and 1930's when the Kingfish governed."[9]

I

All the King's Men is not, however, fictional biography. Warren has dissociated himself from the opinions of the early reviewers who rushed forward to accuse him of writing an "apologia" for Huey Long. Warren is explicit on this point: "Willie Stark was not Huey Long. Willie was only himself, whatever that self turned out to be, a shadowy wraith or a blundering human being."[10] Nevertheless, the externals of Long's career closely parallel those of Willie Stark's. Like Huey Long, Willie Stark comes from a section of a Southern state (never named in the novel) which suddenly prospers with the coming of sawmills, then relapses into poverty after the fields are denuded. Willie, like his prototype, studies late into the night in a Lincolnesque effort at self-education. He earns his living by peddling from door to door a Fix-It-Yourself kit (Long sold a product called Cottalene). The general outline of Long's political career—his grassroots appeal to the rural districts, his development of a political machine, his bodyguards, his impeachment, his senatorial and presidential ambitions—provide a framework story for the novel. Stark's legislative programs—the educational system, highway construction, free medical care, tax reform—are identical with Long's. Finally, the circumstances of the assassination are remarkably similar. The resemblances, however, are only in externals for, as Warren has wisely said, "suggestion does not mean identity, and even if I had wanted to make Stark a projection of Long, I should not have known how to go about it."[11]

In telling the story of the rise and fall of Willie Stark, Warren did not wish to write a "straight naturalistic novel." He felt the "necessity for a character of a higher degree of self-consciousness than my politician, a character to serve as a kind of commentator and *raisonneur* and chorus. . . . So Jack Burden entered the scene."[12]

The Jack Burden we meet in the opening paragraph of the novel is, in many ways, the ideal narrator. He is, first of all, a historian with the historian's devotion to "fact." He is not squeamish about ransacking the "sad detritus of time" which is the "human past" (205). Moreover, Jack loves Truth, loves it voraciously, with a precise, judicious, almost niggling dedication. "It was always that way," he is likely to say, and then, on second thought, to add, "or like that" (156). He has the historian's sensitivity to the impingement of the past on the present, and the substance of the novel consists of three projects of historical research. First, there is the subject of Jack's doctoral dissertation, the journal of Cass Mastern. Second, there is the project of digging up the dirt on Judge Montague Irwin. And finally, there is the novel itself: Jack's reconstruction of his own past and that of Willie Stark.

Jack has another quality which particularly fits him for the role of historian: an insatiable, compulsive curiosity. He is continually seeking the elusive moment of illumination, the "dazzle" which will explain all and justify all. Watching the headlights of his car probing into the night, he ponders on the "blazing" corridor of light which splits the dark in front of him but which, no matter what his speed, remains tantalizingly beyond him. Or crossing the state on a train, Jack sees a sudden flash of sunlight as a woman comes out of her farmhouse door and throws a basin of water to the ground. Watching her return to the house, Jack feels that she must know the answer to a question he cannot even frame.

At the opening of *All the King's Men,* one of the most memorable beginnings in modern American fiction, we not only meet Jack Burden in a characteristic mood, but, as in the opening paragraphs of *Night Rider,* we find in embryo the themes which are developed in the course of the novel. The novel begins, as do so many American novels, on the road. A black, official limousine speeds down the highway, a straight, white, glistening slab with a black line painted down the center. In the car are Governor Willie Stark, his wife Lucy, their son Tom, the Governor's chauffeur and bodyguard Sugar Boy, and Jack Burden, all bound for Willie's birthplace, a poultry farm outside Mason City in the northern section of a Southern state. Jack Burden, his eyes glued to the road, is speculating nervously on the possibilities for disaster for "two tons of expensive mechanism" hurtling down the highway at eighty miles-per-hour: ". . . if you don't quit staring at that line and don't take a few deep breaths and slap yourself hard on the back of the neck you'll hypnotize yourself and you'll come to just at the moment when . . . [the automobile] starts the dive" (3).

The opening paragraphs render with Naturalistic detail the surface and texture of the scene, but the richness of language indicates that the scene carries the additional suggestiveness of symbolism with its literal and latent levels of meaning. The highway is raised to the level of the archetypal symbol of each man's progress through life. The predicament of the narrator is summed up by his preoccupation with the line painted down the center of the highway. The line serves as a guide, a source of direction, yet his single-minded devotion to that line has the effect of mesmerizing him so that he is in danger of being destroyed by the very thing which assures his salvation. This effect is reinforced by the onomatopoeia, achieved by the repetition of coordinate elements in the sentences, which suggests the monotonous whine of the tires and the drone of the engine. The machine, in this case an automobile, is a metaphor that embodies the philosophy of mechanistic determinism which Jack Burden, at this point in his own spiritual odyssey, has adopted. And the car that "whips on into the dazzle" accents the mirage-like quality of the truth which Jack is perpetually seeking, but which remains elusively beyond his reach.

II

A persuasive argument can be made for a "double-hero"[13] in *All the King's Men*. The novel, however, is essentially the story of Jack Burden, and the significance of the life of Willie Stark is ultimately its significance in the life of Jack Burden. The title of the novel shifts the emphasis from the king to his men, and Jack Burden is Willie's man. Jack denies it. He goes to great pains to dissociate himself from the assorted louts and lackies who surround the Governor and relishes those moments when he can look Willie in the eye and threaten to quit. But in a moment of self-betrayal, he humiliates a city policeman and then runs for cover behind the power of Willie Stark. Although Jack is instantly filled with self-loathing, the experience provides a measure of his own attraction to, and corruption by, power. He is caught in a gravitational force which, at once attracting and repelling, holds him within the orbit of Willie Stark. At the end, after the fruits of violence and corruption have been reaped, Jack is still convinced of the Governor's stature: "I must believe that Willie Stark was a great man" (452).

The lives of the two men are inextricably woven. The structure of the opening chapter emphasizes this interrelationship for it divides into two parts, each concerned with the return of a man to the place of his birth. For Willie Stark it is a return to a poultry farm outside Mason City, an eroded land of swamps and scrub pine, Baptist fundamentalism, and grinding poverty. For Jack Burden it is a return to Burden's Landing, a row of handsome estates fronting on the Gulf where the ancestral portraits look down from richly paneled walls. The two experiences lead Jack to speculate on a familiar theme in Southern literature—you can't go home again: "The child comes home and the parents put the hooks in him. . . . It's not love. . . . It is just something in the blood. It is a kind of blood greed" (39). The reactions to the experience of homecoming tell much about the two men. On Willie, the hooks don't snag a thing. "I gotta shove," he says, and shoves. Jack, on the other hand, returns to find himself caught up in old loyalties and obligations which pull him back into the depths of the past. These stirrings of memory lead him to recount, in a series of contrasted scenes, the rise of Willie Stark from hick idealist to ruthless political operator. There is Cousin Willie from the country, circa 1922, wearing Christmas tie and rumpled suit, drinking orange pop and smarting under the jibes of the state auditor, Tiny Duffy. Then there is Governor Stark, circa 1936, wearing tailored clothes, drinking Scotch, and annihilating Lieutenant Governor Duffy with a quip.

Despite Jack Burden's efforts to render precisely the form and pressure of his time, the Willie Stark who emerges from the narrative remains an enigma. Warren has said that behind the novel stand the "scholarly and benign"[14] figure of William James and the "cold-faced Florentine," Machiavelli. Certainly Willie is both coldly pragmatic and engagingly opportunistic. He is more concerned with manipulating the world as he finds it, in a fatalistic and joyous acceptance of things as they are, than in plumbing philosophic depths. His philosophy, which he explains on several occasions, is disarmingly simple. "Badness" is all that exists; one has no choice but to make "goodness" out of it. Willie's simplistic credo, his cheerful acceptance of the in-evitability of evil, offends Jack's feeling for nuance and subtlety; and it fails to satisfy his own curiosity concerning his attraction to Willie. When Jack queries Willie about their relationship, the answer is cryptic: "You work for me because I'm the way I am and you're the way you are" (204). Pressed by Jack to explain, Willie can only reply, "There's something inside you" (278).

Jack's fascination with Willie and his desire to understand that fascination lead him to explore their relationship. Chapters two and three develop, in a series of intricately plotted flash-backs, the educations of the two men. The focus is properly kept on Willie Stark. The story traces the transformation of Cousin Willie, political idealist, into Governor Willie, political realist, and incorporates most of the elements of the Long legend that Warren has chosen to use.

In the course of the exposition, we learn a good deal indirectly about Jack Burden. During the years that he is watching Cousin

Willie being transformed into a Southern Machiavelli, Jack persists in his own "brass-bound" idealism. This idealism is the earliest stage in his spiritual autobiography. It is a philosophy, he tells us, he got from a book in college, but for him it is less a philosophy than a strategy of retreat and withdrawal. ("The world was full of things I didn't want to know" [151].) His history is revealed obliquely in tangled memories and sentimental reveries, but the reason for his malaise gradually emerges. His mother he believes to be a brittle, shallow woman incapable of love. Her husband, Ellis Burden, lives in a slum and distributes religious tracts on street corners. Jack can feel only pity for one and contempt for the other. The woman Jack loves, Anne Stanton, has rejected him because of the apparent purposelessness of his life.

Jack Burden's lip service to idealism is, therefore, largely a sneering distrust of speculative thought, of all formal efforts to explain life. But events, coupled with his inquisitive temperament, force speculation upon him. Each new discovery, each stage in his intellectual and spiritual development, is announced by a Big Sleep, a complete retreat into unconsciousness often accompanied by a flight westward, "drowning in west." The imagery of this process is Freudian in its inspiration and, as Norton Girault has shown in an excellent article,[15] operates as a motif of spiritual death and rebirth. Although living in an atmosphere of political corruption, Jack smugly refuses to believe that he can be contaminated. He shrinks from the awful possibility that he may discover evil within himself. Only by being reborn through a realization of the burden of guilt he shares with all men can he be said to be wholly man.

Jack Burden is a divided man, sick with the "terrible division" of his age. Fragmented himself, he sees the world divided against itself. This division is dramatized by the fact that there are two Jack Burdens, the one who is telling the story and the other to whom the events happened. Such comments as "But that summer from the height of my Olympian wisdom, I seemed to find a great many things funny which now do not appear quite as funny" (338) remind us that time has passed and things are different. The effect is even more emphatically dramatized in the fourth chapter when the point of view shifts radically from the first-person narrator to the third person, and we are introduced to another Jack Burden "of whom the present Jack Burden, *ME*, is a legal, biological, and perhaps even metaphysical continuator" (168). Although the story is apparently told by one person, Warren has actually employed a dual narrator through which the story is refracted. His intricate handling of chronology involves having two and sometimes three levels of time alternately or simultaneously holding the stage, a technique which owes something to Conrad and to Faulkner. The present narrator, moreover, is a conscious artist who withholds information from the reader to kindle suspense and to create anew the shock of discovery. Warren's handling of these points of view, together with his manipulation of chronology, is the great technical triumph of the novel.

Jack Burden's efforts at integration of self are thwarted by his inclination toward abstraction. He generalizes people, including himself, into types. He is the College Boy, the Brass-Bound Idealist, or the Master Mind, behaving and responding in a stereotyped fashion which releases him from the responsibility for his actions. The procession of his mother's husbands includes the Scholarly Attorney, the Tycoon, the Count, and the Young Executive. Adam Stanton, a puzzle to the mature Jack, is understandable as the Friend of His Youth. Even Willie Stark becomes "the Boss," a baffling character in whom Jack "must" believe.

Jack's mind, running as it does to abstraction, tends to polarize terms of thought. He contrasts the urban metropolis of the Capitol with the remote and rural heartland of Mason City and Burden's Landing: one is the world of public affairs; the other, of private experience. These are correlatives for two spheres of sensibility: one of isolation and alienation and the other of stability and meaning.

In a similar fashion, Jack tends to pair off the main figures in the drama. The friend of his youth, Adam Stanton, he comes to call the "man of idea," and the friend of his maturity, Willie

Stark, the "man of fact." Each was doomed to destroy the other, "just as each was doomed to try to use the other and to yearn toward and try to become the other, because each was incomplete with the terrible division of their age" (462). In the same way, Jack contrasts Willie Stark and Tiny Duffy; the two men represent poles in the spectrum of practical politics, and Tiny serves as an alter-ego on whom Willie heaps contempt and insult "because of a blind, inward necessity" (105). Furthermore, Jack sees in Willie a reflection of his own deep-seated division of self. Willie seems always two people: the innocent and idealistic Cousin Willie and the dynamic and masterful Governor. Jack categorizes his two "fathers" as temperamental opposites, Ellis Burden the "good, weak father" and Montague Irwin the "evil, strong one." Jack thinks of his two roommates in graduate school in the same terms: one industrious, stupid, unlucky, and alcoholic and the other idle, intelligent, lucky, and alcoholic. Jack's style is informed by this same division, a mixture of the consciously literary and elegant with the earthy and bawdy.

The pressure of events forces Jack to abandon his position as a brass-bound idealist and to embrace a philosophy which, again with his tendency toward abstraction and generalization, he calls the Great Twitch. Warren has testified to his interest in Naturalistic determinism while at work on the novel,[16] and the Great Twitch is a metaphor for the cluster of ideas associated with that philosophy. For Jack it expresses the mindless, meaningless series of stimuli which provoke an automatic response. Man is but a collection of atoms which spin merrily, or not so merrily. The Great Twitch is the "dream of our age," the dream that all life is but the "dark heave of the blood and the twitch of the nerve" (329). This austere philosophy has its consolations, for it releases the actor from the consequences of his act and makes possible a new "innocence."

The philosophy of the Great Twitch is symbolized in *All the King's Men* by a recurring pattern of machine imagery. This era is, we are told at the beginning of the novel, the "age of the internal combustion engine." Jack's first wife, Lois, he comes to regard as a "sweet-smelling, sweet-breathed machine" (321).

The young Willie Stark, dejected and defeated, wearily paces up and down in his hotel "until the machine wore out" (76). The most elaborate treatment of this idea is the prefrontal lobectomy performed by Dr. Adam Stanton on a catatonic schizophrenic (a mental disease which points to the divided nature of modern man). The operation is carried out with a "contraption like a brace and bit" and a "Gigli saw," tools which give access to the "real mechanism" inside. For Jack it is all "high-grade carpenter work," and he is prompted to baptize the patient in the "name of the Great Twitch" (338). The Great Twitch, the "accident of circumstance," fails eventually to satisfy Jack's needs. And he comes to believe Willie Stark's dying words, "It might all have been different, Jack" (425).

In tracing the stages of Jack Burden's philosophic growth, we come finally to the fact that he is, as he so frequently reminds us, a historian; and it is from his meditations on the past that the inner logic of *All the King's Men* emerges. The formulation of Jack's philosophy of history begins with his first journey into the past—his study of the journal of Ellis Burden's maternal uncle, Cass Mastern. Readers acquainted with the Willie Proudfit episode in *Night Rider* and with the "Statement of Ashby Wyndham" in *At Heaven's Gate* will not be surprised when Warren turns suddenly to a story apparently unrelated to Willie Stark. The Cass Mastern episode, Chapter Four of the novel, is a superb evocation of the ante-bellum South and a bravura piece of imaginative historical reconstruction without equal in American literature. The narrative, in contrast to the complex interweaving of episodes in the narrative of Willie Stark, is chronological. The style, in contrast to the flippant and cynical reportorial style of Jack Burden, is coolly objective.

The story deals with two brothers. Gilbert Mastern, confident and self-contained, serves unscathed throughout the Civil War, loses a fortune in defeat, and recoups it during Reconstruction. Cass Mastern, sensitive and brooding, becomes involved in a love affair with the wife of his best friend, Duncan Trice. Learning of the affair, Trice commits suicide; and his wife, Annabella, in a fit of despondency, blames Cass and dismisses him. Filled with remorse, Cass enters the Confederate Army; marches into battle, refusing to bear arms; and, in the fighting outside Atlanta, finds the bullet he is seeking. From these experiences Burden draws a moral about the nature of the world, a moral which is embodied in the central metaphor of the novel.

> [Cass] learned that the world is like an enormous spider web and if you touch it, however lightly, at any point, the vibration ripples to the remotest perimeter and the drowsy spider feels the tingle and is drowsy no more but springs out to fling the gossamer coils about you who have touched the web and then inject the black, numbing poison under your hide. It does not matter whether or not you meant to brush the web of things. Your happy foot or your gay wing may have brushed it ever so lightly, but what happens always happens and there is the spider, bearded black and with his great faceted eyes glittering like mirrors in the sun, or like God's eye, and the fangs dripping.
> (200)

Jack Burden's initial fascination with the story of Cass Mastern stems from the hope that he may come to know himself through his knowledge of another. Certain parallels encourage him in his quest. Like Cass, Jack is a seeker and a dreamer, oblivious to the fact that actions involve responsibility. By an ironic reversal, Jack has behaved "nobly" with Anne Stanton, yet has "by an obscure and necessary logic" driven her into the arms of Willie Stark. He finds it puzzling that his "nobility" has had a consequence as dire in his world as Cass Mastern's sin had had in his. Jack studies Cass Mastern's intimate journal for eighteen months, scrupulously documents the "facts" of his life, but eventually abandons the project in despair. He finds its meaning only when he sees it in the broader perspective provided by his second research project, undertaken this time on orders from Willie Stark: the search for evidence of corruption in the life of Judge Irwin.

Since Judge Irwin had been the idol of Jack's childhood, Jack undertakes the quest largely to disprove Stark's theory that there is evidence of evil in the life of every man. But Jack's last illusion is shattered; the Judge had once accepted a bribe. Confronted by Jack with the evidence, Irwin takes his own life. The aftermath of the suicide uncovers still another sin. Irwin, like Cass Mastern, had committed adultery with the wife of a trusted friend, Ellis Burden. The consequence in each case was the same—three blighted lives. Thus Jack finds yet another parallel between himself and Cass Mastern: both have hounded a man to suicide. Jack had not meant to touch the web, but it had vibrated to the remotest perimeter.

The image of the spider web serves Jack as an explanation for the assassination of Willie Stark. The question arises, who is responsible for Willie's death? Certainly Willie is partly to blame. Jettisoning the philosophy he has taught Jack, that good and evil are inextricable, Willie determines, after the death of his son, to redirect the course of his life and cleanse his administration. With this attempted return to innocence, Willie is swept down in the avalanche he begins. By banishing the corrupt contractor Gummy Larson, Willie offends Tiny Duffy and brings about the collapse of the political machine. In deciding to return to his wife, from whom he is separated, Willie excites the wrath of his mistress, Sadie Burke, who, years before when he had strayed, had prophesied, "I'll kill him" (150). She thinks of herself as the murderess, but it is Tiny Duffy who has informed Adam Stanton that Willie is having an affair with his sister, Anne. And it is Adam who pulls the trigger. Adam's motive, in the best Southern tradition of honor and violence, is to avenge the defilement of his sister. Tom Stark, the Governor's son, shares in the communal guilt, for his incorrigible behavior, in large part a consequence of his father's indulgence, has inspired Willie to purge himself of evil. Tom, like Jack Burden, cannot be absolved from having caused his father's death. In the widening circle of guilt, Jack sees himself "involved in some monstrous conspiracy."

The cost of making sense out of history has been high, so high in fact that Jack has come to feel that perhaps the only worth-while knowledge is that which "has cost some blood." But, amid the wreckage of so many lives, he is at last ready to frame his philosophy of history. It is found in its most simplified form in a speech to his mother at the conclusion of the novel: "I tried to tell her how if you could not accept the past and its burden there was no future, for without one there cannot be the other, and how if you could accept the past you might hope for the future, for only out of the past can you make the future" (461). This knowledge has been won from his two excursions into the past. From his study of Cass Mastern's journals, Jack has learned the isolation and alienation of the human condition. "It is a human defect," Cass had written, "to try to know oneself by the self of another. One can only know oneself in God and in His great eye" (184). Armed with this knowledge, Jack is ready to accept the insight of Ellis Burden that the separation of man from man is but the imperfect reflection of the separation of man from God.

> Separateness is identity and the only way for God to create, truly create, man was to make him separate from God Himself, and to be separate from God is to be sinful. The creation of evil is therefore the index of God's glory and His power. That had to be so that the creation of good might be the index of man's glory and power. But by God's help.
>
> (462-63)

Jack thus comes to realize the paradox of identity: that knowledge of self consists in a recognition not only of man's isolation but also of the burden of sin that binds all men. Only through acceptance of this dilemma can the split sensibility of modern man hope to achieve integration of self—or, in terms of the novel's title, to put Humpty Dumpty together again. Such spiritual wholeness as is possible for man lies in his capacity for love.[17] "If you loved," Jack says, "and were loved perfectly, then there wouldn't be any difference between the two you's. . . . They would coincide perfectly . . . as when a stereoscope gets the twin images on the card into perfect adjustment" (299). This theme is further reinforced by the epigraph of the novel taken from Dante: "Not by the malediction of bishop or priest is Eternal Love so lost, that it cannot return again, *as long as hope hath still a speck of green.*" Salvation lies in a realm of spirit beyond all the king's horses and all the king's men of this world.

Jack's new-found knowledge is meaningless, however, if it is isolated from the flux of history and raised to a chilly pinnacle of abstraction. The fullness of life can be realized only in the concreteness of the present moment. Jack's immersion in the past has shown him that "meaning is never in the event but in the motion through event" (287). The present moment is the point in time in which the past is made manifest and the future determined. Life is motion, a process not of being but of becoming. Thus a matured and chastened Jack Burden can enter, with Anne Stanton, "the convulsion of the world, out of history into history and the awful responsibility of Time" (464).

III

As Francis Fergusson remarked, *All the King's Men* is constantly threatening to become "a panorama of man-in-society in the grand manner, something comparable to one of Shakespeare's histories."[18] It is one of those rare books that appeal equally to the literary intelligentsia and to the so-called common readers. It shows every sign of possessing remarkable staying power, for it continues to generate intellectual excitement and passionate identification. Certainly no novel written since World War II has surpassed it in technical virtuosity and in philosophic depth. Hollywood has paid it the compliment of an adaptation, and although lacking the thematic richness of the novel, the film was successful enough on cinematic terms to win an Academy Award.

The translation of *All the King's Men* to the screen confirmed Warren's original impulse that the theme lent itself to dramatic treatment. He has, in fact, repeatedly returned to his material to revise it for the stage. The original conception, the verse drama "Proud Flesh," has never been published, although it was produced in April, 1946, at the University of Minnesota where Warren was teaching. Patterned loosely on Greek tragedy,

"Proud Flesh" focuses on a Southern politician of heroic mold, Willie Talos, who falls because of the fatal flaw of hubris. Warren employed a chorus of surgeons who comment on the action, and Jack Burden appears only fleetingly in the closing moments of the play to evoke in the assassin, Keith Amos, the poignant memory of the innocence of their childhood. A second version of the drama, also unpublished, was presented in 1947 by the Dramatic Workshop of the New School for Social Research under the title "All the King's Men." This time Warren substituted a professor of science for the chorus and rewrote and amplified the plot to bring it into closer harmony with the action of the novel.[19] The result was a crowded stage and a complicated narrative line which led Wolcott Gibbs to remark in the *New Yorker* that Warren had "exercised almost no selection, and the unnecessary complex of stories on the stage might easily be quite incomprehensible to anyone who hadn't read the book."[20]

Warren may have agreed with this criticism, for in the third version of the play, produced off-Broadway in October, 1959, and published the following year as *All the King's Men: A Play*, Warren greatly simplified the action, eliminated the choric commentary, and reduced the number of scenes from twenty-four to a prologue and three acts. But whatever the play's merits as theater, it will inevitably be judged against the novel, and that is stiff competition indeed. In the play, Warren employed a character, the "Professor," who, paired with Jack Burden, generates in some measure the tension achieved through the novel's use of a dual narrator. And the play naturally gains impact from the simplicity of plot and the economy of action.

But Warren himself points to the central difficulty of the play in his essay on Joseph Conrad's novel *Nostromo*. Conrad, Warren tells us, wished "to arrive at his meanings immediately, through the sensuous renderings of passionate experience, and not merely to define meanings in abstraction, as didacticism or moralizing."[21] Whereas the meanings of the novel emerge organically from the texture of the experience, the meanings of the drama seem imposed upon the action from without. The characters make their points with a shrill insistence that renders them but shadowy projections of their counterparts in the novel. What Warren achieved in his novel is, to use one of his own favorite words, *inwardness. All the King's Men* is a novel which needs, indeed demands, repeated readings to reveal its richly convolved meanings. In *Night Rider* and *At Heaven's Gate* Warren had demonstrated that he could create incident and character and that he was possessed of a talent which, in its extravagance and gusto, was reminiscent of the Elizabethans. With the publication of *All the King's Men,* it became apparent that his gifts had matured through a rigorous and disciplined apprenticeship to his art. From the Naturalists he had learned the necessity not only of documenting his imaginative world, but also of conceiving it in terms of a philosophic order. From the Symbolists he had learned a technique of endowing his creation with the suggestiveness and depth of human experience. In the fusion of these two traditions Warren has given us in *All the King's Men* a vision of the modern world, startling in its freshness and terrifying in its accuracy.

IV

Robert Penn Warren was engaged in writing *All the King's Men* from the spring of 1943 until the fall of 1945, but his work was frequently interrupted, first by his teaching responsibilities at the University of Minnesota and then, in 1944, by his appointment to the post of Consultant in Poetry at the Library of Congress. Moreover, in keeping with his enormous capacity for work, Warren had undertaken simultaneously with the writing of the novel a critical analysis of Coleridge's *The Ancient Mariner* which appeared in 1946 as the foreword to an edition of the poem. Frederick A. Pottle has described this essay as the "most elaborate and learned critique"[22] Coleridge's poem has ever received, and Richard Harter Fogle has called it a "classic of contemporary appreciation."[23]

Warren's provocative explication of the poem is buttressed by an erudite and searching commentary on Coleridge's philosophic and critical theories. Addressing himself to the critics who have found the poem incoherent, Warren argues for a symbolic reading in terms of a primary theme of the sacramental vision, or the "One Life," and a secondary theme of the imagination, a term Warren asks us to define in the special sense used by Coleridge in his philosophic discourse ("the living power and prime agent of all human perception").

In Warren's reading, the mariner's shooting of the albatross is a symbolic representation of Original Sin, a manifestation of the inscrutable perversity of man's will. The act is devoid of motivation, thus constituting a reenactment of the Fall. The other mariners are implicated in the crime, for they too have violated the sacramental nature of the universe by treating it with indifference. Although the bird is "pious" and of "good omen," the mariners condone the act on practical grounds, "by making man's convenience the measure of his acts." "The Mariner," Warren writes, "shoots the bird; suffers various pains, the greatest of which is loneliness and spiritual anguish; upon recognizing the beauty of the foul sea snakes experiences a gush of love for them and is able to pray; is returned miraculously to his home port, where he discovers the joy of human communion in God, and utters the moral, 'He prayeth best who loveth best, etc.' We arrive at the notion of universal charity . . . the sense of the 'One Life' in which all creation participates."[24] Thus the fable, in Warren's opinion, dramatizes an essentially Christian statement of sin, punishment, repentance, and redemption.

Since Warren was explicating *The Ancient Mariner* at the same time that he was writing *All the King's Men,* it is tempting to speculate on the motives that drew him to Coleridge's poem while he was exploring the themes which form the intellectual structure of the novel. Certainly there are suggestive parallels between the two works. Both are examples of the archetypal story of Rebirth or the Night Journey, and in *All the King's Men* this fable is emphasized by an explicit pattern of imagery. The plight of Jack Burden, and that of Cass Mastern, resembles that of the mariner—"loneliness and spiritual anguish." Also, both Jack and Cass, having achieved a kind of redemption, feel a compulsion to tell their story. The parallel with *The Ancient Mariner* is further enhanced by the marine and nautical imagery which recurs like a leitmotif throughout the novel. And finally, a Coleridgean comment on the will, as quoted by Warren in his essay, could stand as the epigraph to *All the King's Men*: "But in its utmost abstraction and consequent state of reprobation, the will becomes Satanic pride and rebellious self-idolatry in the relations of the spirit to itself, and remorseless despotism relatively to others . . . by the fearful resolve to find in itself alone the one absolute motive of action."[25]

V

Released suddenly from the concentrated work necessary to complete *All the King's Men* and the critical essay on *The Ancient Mariner,* Warren in the spring of 1946 found himself in a retrospective mood. Living in the heart of Minneapolis, a Northern city where snow was still falling in May, he was, as he said, "indulging nostalgia" in recalling the coming of spring in his native Kentucky and Tennessee. The chain of association sparked by those memories led to a short story, "Blackberry Winter," which was published in 1946. It is Warren's masterpiece and one of the great stories of American literature.

The action of the story is simply the events of one morning in the life of a nine-year-old boy who lives on a tobacco farm in rural Tennessee. The surface of each scene is rendered with the pristine freshness it would have for the mind of a sensitive and observant child. The June morning dawns cold and damp, a season called blackberry winter because of its unnatural and unpleasant retrogression from the warmth of spring. The boy, Seth, resents his mother's insistence that he wear shoes that spring morning, for the day promises the excitement of exploration about the farm. A storm the night before, a "gully washer," has flooded the creek, washing out crops and spreading destruction over the countryside.

Each of the apparently trivial details of the boy's excursion about the neighborhood builds toward the moment of illumination. Seth examines the "stringy and limp" bodies of drowned chicks whose eyes have "that bluish membrane over them which makes you think of a very old man who is sick about to die." With a crowd of neighbors, the boy watches a dead cow floating down the creek and listens uncomprehendingly to a veteran of Forrest's cavalry ruminate on human privation. When he goes to the usually immaculate cabin of two Negroes, Dellie and Jebb, to play with their son, Little Jebb, Seth feels some unformulated stirrings of disenchantment when he finds that the storm has washed trash and filth out from under the cabin. The shock of sudden violence intrudes when Dellie, suffering from "woman mizry," cruelly slaps Little Jebb for playing too noisily. When Seth asks Old Jebb for an explanation of Dellie's unaccustomed ill-temper, he replies, "Hit is the change of life and time." The tone of foreboding is enhanced when Old Jebb predicts that "this-here old yearth is tahrd . . . and ain't gonna perduce."

These apparently random incidents are brought suddenly and sharply into focus by Seth's experience with a tramp, a knife-wielding and worthless drifter apparently cast up, like refuse, by the storm. The inquisitive child trails him from the farm, trying to draw him into conversation. Abruptly the tramp turns on him and snarls, "You don't stop following me and I cut yore throat, you little son-of-a-bitch." "But I did follow him," the narrator adds, "all the years."

In the span of a single morning, the child has experienced his own blackberry winter. He has been thrust suddenly and violently from the warmth of his childish innocence to the chill knowledge of the "jags and injustices" of an adult world. Each of the events of the day is a correlative of loss and change, and each is expressed through a series of ironic contrasts: the benevolence and malevolence of nature, the timeless world of the child and the time-obsessed world of the adult, the rooted and intimately familiar farm and the rootless and alien city. Seth tells the story, but what we hear is the memory of that June morning recounted thirty-five years after the event. The man is looking backward on the boy he once was, recalling objectively his childhood bewilderment. The events of the day had puzzled the child, but the man, remembering the experience, is not puzzled. Rather he now sees the experience as a paradigm of a problem he has carried into adulthood. He has come to terms with the problem—it is one mark of his maturity—but it is a problem that is never finally resolved. It is the imaginative awareness of what Warren has called, in speaking of "Blackberry Winter," the "human communion."[26] The narrator of the story recognizes that the brotherhood of man must embrace even the contemptible, cowardly, and defeated tramp of the story; and he grasps the sense of responsibility that such a recognition entails.

"Blackberry Winter" is the finest among the fourteen short stories Warren collected in 1948 under the title *The Circus in the Attic*. The contents of the book go back to 1930 with the inclusion of "Prime Leaf," and several of the stories date from the period of the *Southern Review*.[27] The only story that approaches "Blackberry Winter" in its exercise of creative control over its material, although it is less poignant and universal, is "The Patented Gate and the Mean Hamburger." The resemblances between the two stories may be traced to the fact that both were written in the spring of 1946 when thoughts of his Southern boyhood were much in Warren's mind.

"The Patented Gate and the Mean Hamburger" develops quietly and slowly, seeming at first scarcely a story at all. It describes a type of Tennessee farmer—red-necked, gaunt-faced, tight-lipped—from whom the central character, Jeff York, differs only in his modest prosperity. The symbol of his years of sweat and deprivation is a patented gate, an elaborate contraption of crossbars and braces operated mechanically, which opens to his dirt farm. Stroke by stroke, a portrait is built up of the people who inhabit the nearby town where Jeff, his wife, and their children spend each Saturday afternoon: the citified and contemptuous owner of a diner, Slick Hardin; the snickering townsfolk sitting at his counter munching their hamburgers; the condescending bank president, Todd Sullivan. Forced by his wife to sell his farm and buy Slick Hardin's diner, Jeff York stoically establishes her in town. Then, without a word, he walks out to his farm and hangs himself from the patented gate. The story is narrated by an anonymous spokesman for the town, and from the opening sentence ("You have seen him a thousand times") we are made gradually aware that the members of the community, despising as they do hick dumbness, are inescapably involved in the suicide of Jeff York.

The story from which the collection takes its title, "The Circus in the Attic," returns to the Bardsville of *Night Rider,* ranging backward to the founding of the village and its part in the Civil War and forward to the slum-ridden, factory town of the present. The plot chronicles the life of Bolton Loveheart, a mother-dominated and bloodless town aristocrat who finds meaning in his later years by idealizing his stepson, a Medal of Honor hero of World War II. Certain scenes in the story are vintage Warren: the evocation of the town's history, the death of Bolton's mother, the hilarious recounting of a Yankee raid by the town derelict. A rambling and diffuse story, it seems more a synopsis of a Warren novel than a fully realized short story.

"The Circus in the Attic," in fact, points to a weakness in many of the stories included in this collection. The prodigality of Warren's talent, his gift for sustained narrative and invention, seems cramped within the confines of the short story. He has written nothing in the form since 1946, and in an autobiographical note on the writing of "Blackberry Winter," he bade farewell to the genre.[28] How far the form of the short story was from satisfying his artistic needs may be surmised by the fact that, while collecting his short stories in 1948, he was hard at work on his longest and most complex novel, *World Enough and Time,* which appeared in the spring of 1950.

CHAPTER 5

The Detritus of History

IN *World Enough and Time* the full-dress documentation of the past in the manner of the Cass Mastern episode in *All the King's Men* is expanded to an entire novel. Following as it did the critical and popular success of *All the King's Men*, *World Enough and Time* appears, in the Warren canon, to be an attempt at a magnum opus. In writing this novel Robert Penn Warren perhaps intended—as he said Joseph Conrad intended in *Nostromo*—"to create a great, massive, multiphase symbol that would render his total vision of the world, his sense of individual destiny, his sense of man's place in nature, his sense of history and society."[1]

Despite the radical shift to a remote time and place, *World Enough and Time* is an elaboration and extension of themes already dealt with in *All the King's Men*. The plot concerns the murder by Jeremiah Beaumont of a politician and lawyer, Colonel Cassius Fort. In Fort, as in Willie Stark, good and evil are inextricably mixed. The narrator of the novel asks: "If Fort did good, could that wipe out his evil?" (132). "He was good," another character adds, "but his good is mixed up with his foulness" (434). Again like Stark, Fort is destroyed by the Southern tradition of personal honor and violence. The responsibility for Fort's death spreads throughout *World Enough and Time,* just as the responsibility for Stark's death spreads throughout *All the King's Men,* staining each of the major characters. In the later novel Warren has concentrated on the "innocent" idealist, Jeremiah Beaumont, who, like Adam Stanton, does the deed and, in so doing, is used by a world he does not understand. Jeremiah bears a relationship to Jack Burden as well: like Jack, he must tell his story and in the telling, try to reconcile the worlds of fact and idea.

In his three earlier novels Warren had written of worlds he had known or seen, but *World Enough and Time* is set in the early years of the nineteenth century. His inspiration was a pamphlet which Katherine Anne Porter showed him in 1944 when both were fellows at the Library of Congress. "I read it in five minutes," Warren said, "but I was six years making the book."[2] Published in Bloomfield, Kentucky, in 1826, and entitled "The Confession of Jereboam O. Beauchamp," the pamphlet is the chief document in an ancient and celebrated murder-seduction story—the Sharp-Beauchamp case—which has held a continuing fascination for American writers. In the 1830's it formed the basis of plays by Edgar Allan Poe, Thomas Holly Chivers, and Charlotte Barnes. Charles Fenno Hoffman incorporated some of the elements of the tale into his romance *Greyslaer,* and William Gilmore Simms stayed closer to the facts as known in *Charlemont* and in its sequel, *Beauchampe.*

The original story is compounded of high tragedy and farce comedy, innocence and corruption, honesty and duplicity. A young attorney, Jereboam O. Beauchamp, heard the story of the seduction and betrayal of Ann Cook by the solicitor-general of Kentucky, Colonel Solomon P. Sharp. Beauchamp impetuously sought her out and proposed marriage, but she would consent only on condition that he vow to murder Sharp. Although Beauchamp was an acquaintance of Sharp and easily provoked a quarrel, Sharp repeatedly refused to accept a challenge. The lovers then conspired together to murder Sharp, and Jereboam stabbed him to death on the night of November 6, 1825. Beauchamp was arrested and pleaded not guilty, but he was convicted after a trial which was marked by corruption on both sides. Although the grand jury had released Ann, she joined Jereboam in his cell where they awaited the day of execution by composing prayers and poems, singing hymns, and making love. When the governor refused a plea for pardon, they attempted to commit suicide by taking laudanum the night before the execution was to take place. When this failed, Jereboam stabbed Ann to death and wounded himself; but he lived long enough to be hanged the following day.

The story has all the trappings of unabashed melodrama—innocence violated, villainy triumphant, honor avenged—and Warren has remained remarkably faithful to both the letter and spirit of his sources.[3] Yet it is precisely because of his gaudy materials that Warren has chosen to remove us two steps from the action through his handling of the point of view. The novel begins:

> I can show you what is left. After the pride, passion, agony, and bemused aspiration, what is left is in our hands. . . . Here is the manuscript he himself wrote, day after day, as he waited in his cell, telling his story. . . . To whom was he writing, rising from his mire or leaning from his flame to tell his story? The answer is easy. He was writing to us.

At once we are introduced to the narrator-historian, the "I" of the story, who has diligently searched out and now displays, often with the professional flourish of the guild historian, the assembled documents. He continually interjects himself to parade the sources, sift the evidence, and analyze the motives. He is forever at the reader's elbow, gently pointing the path through a maze of contradictory testimony, hinting at the need for both detachment and sympathy, reminding him of the contemporary relevance of the events. The code duello, for example, may seem to the sophisticate a quaint and rather fatuous contest between "dunces," but the narrator muses on its modern equivalent: "We do not stand up at dawn, but we lie in a scooped-out hole in a tropical jungle and rot in the rain and wait for the steel pellet whipping through the fronds. . . . we ride a snarling motor into the veil of flak" (128).

Such a technique at first seems a flagrant violation of tone. Warren knew he was sacrificing immediacy, the illusion of entering a place remote in time and temper (although it must be said that there are scenes in this novel—Jeremiah's meeting with the Grand Boz, for example—which are as fully realized as any in American fiction). His method could easily stultify the narrative, as it stultifies so much contemporary historical writing. But the esthetic distance Warren gains is actually a way of framing his materials and of giving verisimilitude to events which contain a large element of the absurd. The narrator-historian also supplies an ironic corrective to any hint of antiquarian condescension, "the sad and contemptuous distance with which we now regard . . . an attic trunk" (52).

The chief document on which the narrator-historian can draw is the manuscript journal of Jeremiah Beaumont, written in his jail cell while he was awaiting execution for the murder of Colonel Fort. The journal is not a diary, a day-by-day account of the experience as it happened, but a recollection of the events and a meditation on their significance. Some readers will not find the overwrought and turgid style of the journal to their taste, but it is completely in character with its author. For Jeremiah, his story is heroic drama, full of "noble gestures and swelling periods, serious as blood" (5). The drama metaphor, occasionally couched in allegorical terms, is sustained throughout the journal; and, the narrator suggests, it was perhaps a drama Jeremiah "had to prepare in order to live at all, or in order, living, to be human" (5). Jeremiah's romantic view of life, a view of "high sentiment and beauty," a muddled mixture formed from his reading of Plato and Byron, cannot stand the test of exposure to the realities of his world.

> So after the fine speeches and the tragic stance, the grand exit was muffed. The actors trip on their ceremonial robes, even at the threshold of greatness, and come tumbling down in a smashing pratt-fall, amid hoots and howls from the house, and the house gets its money's worth. . . . It knows where reality abides: in the femur cracked and the buttocks black and blue.
> (442)

The characters had cast themselves in roles which they were ill-suited to play. They had failed to see that their vision of their destiny was subject to the whim and caprice of others, each of whom was intent on his own private drama.

Jeremiah's failure is his inability to prepare his drama for the two "worlds" with which he must deal. There is the "secret world," subjective, private, ideal; and there is the public world of events, of history, of law and justice. In the Conrad essay already quoted, Warren has said, "Man is precariously balanced in his humanity between the black inward abyss of himself and the black outward abyss of nature."[4] Jeremiah Beaumont is poised just at this point. It is in the tension generated between these two worlds that the novel has its being, and it is in the resolution of this tension that it finds its meaning.

Jeremiah Beaumont is yet another Warren character seeking self-knowledge, hoping to find his identity through the exploration of his private world. "Oh, what am I?" he asks (295), echoing Sue Murdock in *At Heaven's Gate*. And like Jerry Calhoun and Jack Burden, he repeats his name in astonishment, trying to find some connection between the mysterious syllables and his identity. "I am Jeremiah Beaumont, I am Jeremiah Beaumont. But I marveled even at the sound of my name" (393).

The possibility for identity lies in knowledge—of the self and of the world. Jeremiah's search leads him, like Jerry Calhoun, to wish for the death of a parent that he might be released to enjoy worldly success. His search leads him to betray the teacher of his youth, Dr. Leicester Burnham, and the benefactor of his young manhood, Colonel Cassius Fort. Jeremiah drives to suicide the woman he would avenge, Rachel Jordan. And, ultimately, he finds that "the crime for which I seek expiation is never lost. . . . It is the crime of self, the crime of life. The crime is I" (504-5).

Jeremiah's path to this conclusion Warren gives us with an abundance of detail and commentary which is initially absorbing but eventually tedious. The youth of Jeremiah is portrayed against a background of frontier Kentucky during the early nineteenth century. He is a stiff-necked, aloof young man whose natural shyness preserves his innocence in a society both coarse and brutal. He prefers *Pilgrim's Progress* and Franklin's *Autobiography* to the "brightness of the moment and the tickle of the flesh" (45). His bookish tastes encourage in him a fatal tendency to "cast a passion over the commonness of things" (10). His youthful idealism causes him to reject outright the estate of his maternal grandfather, Morton Marcher, when the offer is made on the condition that he take the old man's name. Identity is not that simple.

Jeremiah undergoes a religious conversion in the best frontier-revival fashion, but his exaltation in his new found grace leads him to a frenzied, brutal copulation with a hag lurking on the edges of a clearing. The experience has its analogue in a youthful memory of an illustration from the *Book of Martyrs,* "the picture of a young woman tied cruelly to a post 'so that the bonds seemed to crush her sweet flesh and her face lifted up while the flames rose above her'" (11). Staring at the picture, he is torn between a desire to rescue her from the flames and a desire to light the fire himself. The picture becomes a kind of paradigm of his relationship with Rachel Jordan and of his meditations on the "paradox and doubleness of life" (114).

Having watched his father die "in the bitterness of worldly failure," Jeremiah determines to carve out a better world for himself. The favorite of his schoolmaster, Dr. Burnham, Jeremiah obtains through him the offer of a place in the law office of Colonel Cassius Fort. When the death of his mother releases him from a filial obligation, he comes under the influence of Fort who is "like a father" to him. The relationship of Jeremiah Beaumont and Cassius Fort (like that of Percy Munn and Senator Tolliver, Jerry Calhoun and Bogan Murdock, Jack Burden and Willie Stark) is one in which an older man, paternal and self-assured, takes as an apprentice a callow but promising youth. Warren parallels the growth of friendship between the two men with the growth of intimacy between Fort and Rachel Jordan. She, too, has recently lost her father and has fallen easily under Fort's spell. There follows the development of confidence in Fort, his seduction of Rachel, and Jeremiah's consequent disillusionment.

Inflamed by a Byronic sense of chivalry, Jeremiah lays siege to Rachel's castle ("the princess chained and enchanted"), forces her to tell him of her seduction and the loss of her stillborn child, and wrings from her the command, "Kill Fort!" To Rachel, Jeremiah vows, "We will make what world we will" (79). He longs to commit what he calls the "gratuitous act," the act outside the motives of the world; for, in so doing, he can define himself. Fort becomes "an abstraction." To kill him is to commit "the perfect act, outside the world, pure and untarnished. . . . the perfect justice self-defining and since defining self, defining all else" (181).

Fort refuses Jeremiah's challenge, even when threatened with horsewhipping in the streets. He flees Frankfort where Jeremiah has sought him out, then finds business which keeps him in the East for months. While he is away, the death of Rachel's mother opens the way for Jeremiah and Rachel to marry at once. With Fort out of sight and out of mind, Jeremiah turns to the cultivation of his wife's farm; and, as he constructs the world he had promised her, it brings them, out of fortuitous circumstance, happiness.

In talking of the novel, Warren has said: "I began to think of the political struggle of the time as a kind of mirror I could hold up to the personal story."[5] So with Fort in the wings, Warren shifts the political turmoils of Kentucky to stage center. The struggle is an economic one, an effort on the part of the New Court party to ease the plight of debtors even at the risk of subverting both courts and constitution. The Old Court party is dedicated to sanctity of contract and preservation of the Constitution. The dilemma is an ancient one: is the law manipulative, a pragmatic servant to man's needs ("Where is the voice of Justice but in the belly?"), or is the law a set of enduring, transcendent principles ("Where was the voice of Justice but in the heart?") It is the theme stated in the epigraph to the novel taken from Spenser's *Faerie Queene*: "When Justice was not for most meed outhyred,/But simple Truth did rayne, and was of all admyred."

Although Jeremiah's opinions on the political question are characteristically divided, he is drawn into the campaign on the side of New Court by a friend, Wilkie Barron, whose surname suggests both his spiritual emptiness and his lordly mastery of his world. The occasion of Jeremiah's entry into politics is an election-day riot in which Old Court partisans attempt to prevent Barron's political associate, Percival Skrogg, from voting. Skrogg is gaunt, tubercular, fanatical, indifferent to the flesh and dispassionately devoted to the "idea"—in this case, the New Court. (The narrator underlines the contemporary parallel by pausing to remind us that such doctrinaire liberals are "the glory and the horror of our time.") Seeing Skrogg abused by superior force, Jeremiah leaps quixotically to his defense, an action as uncalculated and selfless as his defense of Rachel Jordan.

Skrogg and Barron are projections of the two worlds Jeremiah would reconcile. They are, respectively, the man of idea and the man of fact, emblems of the "terrible division" delineated in *All the King's Men*. Where Skrogg is unworldly, Wilkie comes of a race possessing "total confidence in the world." Together they can seize and mold their world, making Jeremiah their tool; isolated, each is a doomed man. Skrogg discovers that the idea is not enough—at his death he is found to have made his concession to the terrors of the world. Despite his apparent fearlessness, he wore beneath his threadbare shirt a vest of chain mail. "At some point," the narrator remarks, "he had discovered that he was part of the world, after all, and that the pitiful body he wore was part of himself and precious. More precious than any idea" (94). Wilkie discovers that the world is not enough—"One morning he stepped into his bath . . . and shot himself tidily through the heart, without a single spatter of blood on the floor. Nobody knew why he did it" (509).

Skrogg and Barron draw Jeremiah into the campaign and into the public world of politics. He runs for the state legislature on a New Court platform. In a nearby county, Colonel Fort is running on the opposing ticket. When the story of Fort's seduction of Rachel is introduced into the campaign, the memory of Jeremiah's vow is forced upon him. His efforts to withdraw from life, to purify his idea in the flame of privacy ("the bright, secret center of life") fail abysmally. The narrator traces his efforts to enter into a larger world, the dawning upon him of the purpose that "you had to show the world in the world's way":

Because the world had seemed nothing, he had lived in the way of the world, feeling safe because he held the idea, pure, complete, abstract, and self-fulfilling. He had thought that he was redeemed by the idea, that sooner or later the idea would redeem the world.

But now he knew: the world must redeem the idea.

(228)

And so he radically changes his strategy: "I would submit the idea to the way of the world" (233).

Persuading himself that to kill Fort publicly would be but to indulge his vanity, Jeremiah prepares an elaborate plot and, under cover of darkness, murders Fort in Frankfort. Jeremiah returns triumphant to Rachel. Brought back to Frankfort for trial, he is defended by Madison of New Court and Hawgood of Old Court, two lawyers drawn with an almost allegorical symmetry: "they stood together, the heavy-fleshed, full-blooded seasoned campaigner, and the Platonic student with the thin, sharp, assymmetrical face" (410). The trial becomes a political contest in which Jeremiah, who would have spurned the world, is swept up by its inexorable forces. He is caught up in a tangled web of truth and half-truth, lie and counter-lie. Witnesses are suborned and, in turn, betray their suborners. The scales are tipped against him when Wilkie Barron, fearing the crime will be given a political interpretation and destroy the New Court party, testifies to the motive of personal vengeance. All appeals fail, as does the suicide pact of Rachel and Jeremiah.

At this point in the narrative Warren departs from his sources in the Kentucky Tragedy and has Jeremiah enter on a third stage in his search for identity. Wilkie Barron concocts an escape plan, and Rachel and Jeremiah flee westward to merge into the forests beyond the frontier. Here begins the wierdest tale Warren has given us. It is the story of La Grand' Bosse, a river pirate of almost mythical proportions, who has created by sheer animal force and cunning a community in the heart of the wilderness. The structure of *World Enough and Time* here parallels the two novels that preceded it. In *At Heaven's Gate* Warren had depicted two "worlds," the public world of Bogan

Murdock and the private world of Slim Sarrett, only to throw them both into relief by the delineation of still a third world, that of Ashby Wyndham. In *All the King's Men* the two spheres of action of the novel are put into perspective when seen in contrast with the story of Cass Mastern. By turning to the world of La Grand' Bosse in *World Enough and Time,* Warren gains a similar effect.

For Jeremiah, the journey westward is a flight out of time and into nature; he determines "to deny the idea and its loneliness and embrace the world as all" (505). What is left is a mindless and furious descent into the mire of bestiality. Rachel's mind breaks under the strain, and she commits suicide by stabbing herself in the breast, a symbolic reenactment of Fort's murder and a gesture of expiation for her guilt. Jeremiah, diseased and despairing, intends finally to return to Frankfort to give himself up, but he is denied even that satisfaction. He is murdered on the trail by an accomplice in the plot against him who now seeks the reward for his capture.

Such, in broad outline, is the fable, but, as Warren has said, fable is but "symbol for exfoliating theme."[6] The theme of *World Enough and Time* is articulated through the interpenetration of the two worlds of the novel: one, of external action; the other, of private experience. The meaning consequent upon the interaction of these spheres of sensibility is manifested in the novel by another antithesis—the clearing and the forest. At the center of the novel is the order man has managed to wrest from chaos, the small clearing of the frontiersman. On the periphery is the encroaching forest, the implacable and lawless forces which threaten on all sides. Clearing and forest are symbols for the inner division of self:

> The two worlds impinged, overlay and lapped, blurred and absorbed, twisted together and dissolved like mist. . . . It was a nightmare in which the two worlds, the secret and the public, merged and overlapped and intertwined, their happy doubleness betrayed, betraying him. When they merged and their sharp distinction was lost, you were lost, too.
>
> (333-35)

Man's best effort must be to try to reconcile these two aspects of his nature. He is groping toward knowledge of both worlds in order to bring them into harmony; and, since the process is an organic one, it is doomed by the nature of things to incompleteness. For to realize complete fulfillment would be non-being or death. Singularly enough, it is the victim, Colonel Cassius Fort, who most firmly grasps this insight. Writing to Rachel in extenuation of his conduct, he describes the dichotomy: "I betrayed you and betrayed others who trusted me, compounding betrayal by betrayal, and for those months I lived in a dream outside the hard world and its duties. Then I came back into the world, and hope to do my duty still, whatever it may be and bear with fortitude the ills and losses" (147).

Finally, man has no choice but to endure, to attempt to create a world he can never fully understand. As the narrator observes, "Jeremiah Beaumont had to create his world or be the victim of a world he did not create." He is, however, both creator *and* victim, victim of the world he did create. Even if Jeremiah could gain the knowledge he seeks from a repudiation of the world, there exists the final paradox that his knowledge must be placed "in the context of the world that it repudiated." As the speaker makes plain in Andrew Marvell's "To His Coy Mistress," there is not world enough and time; man must seize on the present moment and wrest from it what significance he can. Such a conclusion veers close to nihilism, but while the speaker in the poem faces this bleak prospect with gaiety and wit, the narrator of the novel speaks in stark and somber tone. The single possibility of affirmation in the novel is voiced by Jeremiah's jailer, Munn Short. Like Willie Proudfit in *Night Rider*, Munn Short had traveled to the West and, in a series of adventures on the trail, had experienced a spiritual death and rebirth, achieving something akin to the sacramental vision of life. But Munn Short's affirmation makes no impression on Jeremiah Beaumont. Nor is it singled out by the narrator for special emphasis. At the end of *World Enough and Time*, he merely repeats Jeremiah's own final question: "Was all for nought?"

As a final gloss on the novel, we have Warren's comment

on Joseph Conrad: "Wisdom, then, is the recognition of man's condition, . . . living with the ever renewing dilemma of idea as opposed to nature, morality to action, justice to material interests. . . . Man must make his life somehow in the dialectical process of these terms, and in so far as he is to achieve redemption he must do so through an awareness of his condition that identifies him with the general human communion, not in absfraction, not in mere doctrine, but immediately. The victory is never won, the redemption must be continually re-earned."[7]

I

While serving as consultant in poetry at the Library of Congress in 1944, the same year that Katherine Anne Porter had shown him the *Confession of Jereboam Beauchamp,* Robert Penn Warren was investigating another sensational episode in the Kentucky history of the nineteenth century—the brutal ax-murder of a Negro slave by Lilburn Lewis, the nephew of Thomas Jefferson. Having heard a folk version of the tale during his boyhood, Warren, from the files of newspapers and the Abolition literature in the Library of Congress and from Kentucky courthouse records, gradually pieced together the facts of the episode. The story is, as he said, a "shocker."[8]

During the first decade of the nineteenth century, Thomas Jefferson's brother-in-law, Dr. Charles Lewis, moved from his tidewater Virginia home with his wife, their two sons, and a number of slaves to western Kentucky. There on a bluff overlooking the confluence of the Ohio and Cumberland rivers, he built an elaborate house, "Rocky Hill." When his wife, Lucy, died soon after the move, Dr. Lewis returned to Virginia, leaving his sons, Lilburn and Isham, to manage Rocky Hill. On the night of December 15, 1811, having first assembled his slaves in the meathouse to witness what he was going to do, Lilburn butchered a slave named George for the trivial offense of breaking a favorite pitcher of Lucy Lewis. On the same December night as the murder, the first of a series of earthquakes shook the Mississippi Valley, and for years afterwards God-fearing people pointed to the coincidence as an instance of Divine displeasure.

News of the crime soon leaked out, and the two brothers were arrested and indicted for murder. While at liberty awaiting trial, they made a pact to shoot each other at their mother's grave. For some reason unknown to history, their plans went awry. Lilburn was killed at the grave edge, but Isham escaped into the wilderness. Although he was apprehended, tried, and sentenced to hang for the murder of Lilburn, Isham somehow contrived his escape and, three years later, was reported killed at the Battle of New Orleans, one of the two Americans lost at that engagement. In 1953 Warren published his version of the story under the title *Brother to Dragons: A Tale in Verse and Voices.*

The tale contained a number of elements calculated to attract Warren: a basis in historical fact, a violent murder, a tangled skein of motivation, and an episode obscured by the mists of time. The crime was bloody and bizarre, but its very monstrousness provided an opportunity for the clearest statement of what, in retrospect, emerges as *the* Warren theme: "All life lifts and longs toward its own name,/And toward fulfillment in the singleness of definition" (121).

For Warren the special appeal of the story was its connection with Thomas Jefferson, the fact that "the philosopher of our liberties and the architect of our country and the prophet of human perfectibility had this in the family blood."[9] And, for the writer absorbed with the problem of self-definition, the career of Jefferson possesses a special appropriateness. It is possible to argue, as Warren has, that it was Jefferson who defined, once and for all, the national character: "We suddenly had to define ourselves and what we stood for in one night. No other nation ever had to do that. In fact, one man did it— one man in an upstairs room, Thomas Jefferson."[10]

For nine years Warren was haunted by the story as he searched for a form adequate to his theme. The form of *Brother to Dragons* is unique, a kind of verse novel, the end-product of a series of mutations. Warren had first thought of a novel but had decided that the story lacked the inevitability of narrative line necessary for the closed form of a novel. He feared that the enigma at the heart of the story would require a burden of commentary too heavy for the almost anecdotal nature of the plot. Warren and a collaborator began to fashion out a play in which Jefferson would have a choric role, but this plan too had to be abandoned because the role of Jefferson tended to overwhelm the material. The problem of finding an appropriate form even makes its way into the poem itself. The author, speaking as the character "R.P.W.," explains that he once intended to make a ballad of the story

> but the form
> Was not adequate: the facile imitation
> Of a folk simplicity would never serve,
> For the beauty of such simplicity is only
> That the action is always and perfectly self-contained, . . .
>
> (43)

"Then, at last," Warren said in a note on the composition of the poem, "I struck on the notion of using the form of a dramatic dialogue—not a play but a dialogue of all the characters, including Jefferson, at some unspecified place and time."[11] The idea of a dramatic dialogue with the setting—as the author's prefatory note informs us—"no place," and the time, "no time," opened up several possibilities. It allowed the author to "get out of the box of mere chronology" and to assess the meaning of the events not in a time-order of history but under the aspect of eternity. By considering the events out of time, Warren could also broaden the perspective to include commentary defining the meaning of the events for the modern world.

Jefferson is, as Warren has said, "the real protagonist."[12] Of course, the introduction of a character of Jefferson's stature would almost certainly dominate any work in which he appeared, for his niche in the American pantheon is firmly fixed and his character is indelibly etched upon the American imagination. To dare to put words into the mouth of the "spiritual father" of America would invite the criticism that a Founding Father would never talk in such a fashion—and such a criticism was promptly made. But if Warren has not written in a spirit of debunking, neither has he written out of a desire to whitewash the American past. Cutting short a satiric aside on the Daughters of the American Revolution, he dismisses the super-patriots in the only couplet in the poem: "But let that pass, for to the pious mind/Our history's nothing if it's not refined" (21). Jefferson speaks less than one-eighth of the lines in the poem and is seldom mentioned by the characters directly involved in the tragedy, yet his shadow falls ominously across the action, darkening and deepening its significance.

The Jefferson of Warren's poem had lived by a majestic dream of the perfectibility of man. He had been heartened by his belief in man's "natural innocence" which, released from its bondage to nature, would "dance like sunlight over the delighted landscape" (41). As a delegate to the Continental Congress, he had transcended self in the ecstasy of composing the Declaration of Independence and, effaced by a self-consuming flame, had seen man "angelic, arrogant, abstract" (9). For Jefferson, "blind with light" from the dazzling brilliance of his theory of human grandeur, the Maison Carreé at Nîmes is the symbol of the rational, balanced, and chaste beauty of the human mind, while the medieval cathedral, adorned with contorted and grotesque images of the human spirit, is a mere aberration of the "Gothic dark." But Lilburn's deed forces him to abandon his "outrageous dreams" and to conclude that "There's no forgiveness for our being human./It's the inexpugnable error" (24).

Warren shows us the element of pride ("that flame in the personal darkness") in Jefferson's nature which is his tragic flaw. He speaks of "my West" and likens himself to a latter-day Moses destined to see that promised land only from afar. Because he is unprepared for the knowledge of man's, and particularly his kinsman's, capacity for evil, his reaction to Lilburn's deed is shrill and furious, his earlier excessive optimism now inverted into a bleak pessimism. The awareness of man's essential evil turns human warmth into a delusion, love into a mask of mockery hiding the "immitigable ferocity of self," and life into the "unsummerable arctic of the human alienation" (47). In his extremity of rage and grief, Jefferson asserts that he would have murdered Lilburn with the same ease that Lilburn murdered the Negro slave, George. "The death of that black boy," Jefferson confesses, "was the death/Of all my hope" (132). Now, out of time and able to contemplate the sweep of American history, Jefferson can find abundant evidence to sustain his new pessimism: the appalling slaughter of the Civil War, the labor warfare at Haymarket Square and Detroit, the perversion of justice in the Sacco-Vanzetti case.

Although Jefferson dominates *Brother to Dragons* by virtue of his massive historical reputation, almost half the lines and most of the interpretative commentary are spoken by the author. The poet, R.P.W. ("red-headed, freckled, lean, a little stooped"), is, of course, a persona, yet there is evidently a large admixture of autobiography in the characterization. While it is always a reckless assumption to identify an author with his creation, even when, as in this case, the name is the same, it would nevertheless appear that *Brother to Dragons* is more personal than any of Warren's preceding works. R.P.W. shares with an entire gallery of Warren characters the need "to be reconciled to the father's own reconciliation" (28). In a varied career he has been a "strayer and stranger" in many nations, and he has "shared the most common/Human experience which makes all mankind one"—isolation. R.P.W. finds mirrored in the story a reflection of his own struggle for meaning and fulfillment even though it is Jefferson who, like the Ancient Mariner in Warren's interpretation, re-enacts the drama of repentance and rebirth. Within the poem the character of R.P.W. functions, in Warren's words, as a "kind of interlocutor," a center around which the action revolves and a focal point for its meaning. Like Jack Burden in *All the King's Men* and the narrator-historian in *World Enough and Time*, R.P.W. carefully culls the documents, sifts the facts from the folksay, and meditates on the ultimate meaning of the events. His manner is generally unassuming and deferential. His voice is subtly modulated, at times colloquial and racy, at others rising to a sweeping and impassioned rhetoric rich with echoes of Shakespeare and Milton. R.P.W. is, in short, part prompter, part commentator, and part participant in the action.

The controlling image of the poem is stated by Jefferson in one of his early speeches:

> The beast waits. He is the infamy of Crete.
> He is the midnight's enormity. He is
> Our brother, our darling brother. And Pasiphaë
> Pasiphaë, huddled and hutched in the cow's hide,
> Laced, latched, thonged up, and humped for joy,
> What was the silence then before the stroke?
> And then your scream.
>
> (7-8)

In the Greek myth, Pasiphaë became enamored of a bull and indulged her unnatural passion in a wooden cow built for her by Daedalus. The offspring of this union, the Minotaur, was half man and half bull. This terrible creature, housed in the Labyrinth, was eventually slain by Theseus.

The Minotaur-Labyrinth image expresses precisely the relationship of man to nature and of man to himself which is central to the theme of the poem. Each man is a labyrinth of his own devising, lost "in some blind lobby, hall, enclave,/ Crank cul-de-sac, couloir, or corridor of time./Of Time. Or self" (7). And within each man there lurks a minotaur, symbol of the bestial and monstrous connection of man with brute nature which he, like Theseus, must slay. As Pasiphaë satisfies her passion in a wooden cow, so man himself is trapped by his passion in an "infatuate machine" of his own invention.

Jefferson, bemused by his conception of natural innocence, had denied man's roots in nature. He had believed that "Man must redeem Nature" (37). R.P.W., however, accepts the familiar dualism of man's nature, Pascal's ape and angel, Swift's Yahoo and Houyhnhnm. At the mythological level, this evil is the bestial in man; at the anagogical level, it is his sin, his Original Sin. Man is, as the author of the Book of Job asserts, a brother to dragons. For R.P.W. man's link with nature is his opportunity for identity. To sink into nature is to sacrifice identity; to be separate from nature is to achieve identity. Man must redeem not nature but himself; and, paradoxically, the cost of his redemption is isolation. "How can there be/Sensation," R.P.W. asks, "where there is perfect adjustment?"

> The blood
> Of the creature is but the temperature of the sustaining flow:
> The catfish is in the Mississippi and
> The Mississippi is in the catfish and
> Under the ice both are at one with God.
> Would that we were!
>
> (94)

Like the catfish, Lilburn has merged his identity with nature. At the moment of the savage act, he abjures his humanity and appears, like the earthquake which shakes the Mississippi Valley the same night, an unleashed force of nature, "mindless, irreconcilable, absolute" (95).

We never hear Lilburn's own account of his actions. The two central figures in the drama, Lilburn and George, each speak only once in the poem. Lilburn utters a plaintive cry, a lament for the loss of light in the encompassing darkness; George gives voice to his agony and bewilderment in the face of the event: "I was lost in my anguish, and I did not know the reason" (194). Victor and victim, then, are left purposely in shadow (indeed, the question arises, who *is* victor and who victim); and the meaning of the murderous act becomes the multiple-truths of the participants who join in the reconstruction of the event.

As each character re-lives his part in the drama, it becomes apparent that the bloody act of hate has somehow stemmed from insufficient or excessive love. Lilburn, who stands at the center of the story, is beloved by all his immediate family, yet their love has not brought him salvation. His mother loved him, but in some obscure way she knows she has failed him. "The human curse," she concludes, "is simply to love and sometimes to love well,/But never well enough" (23). Lilburn's love for her is a "black need," an obsession which is at the root of his tangled dreams and perverse desires. His wife,

Laetitia, loves him, but he brutally defiles her by some unnamed and bestial perversion which shocks and disgusts her. Laetitia, however, has also proved inadequate to the demands of love. Like Pasiphaë "huddled and hutched in the cow's hide," she had hungered for Lilburn. Therefore, in partially willing the act, she must share the responsibility for her own violation. Lilburn's brother, Isham, "just loved Big Bubber" with mute adoration, but Lilburn returns his love with carefully measured abuse and humiliation, saving Isham for the final betrayal at the grave's edge. Aunt Cat, Lilburn's Negro Mammy, loves him with a grim possessiveness and supernal cunning. Lilburn's rejection of her love leads her to betray him to the sheriff ("Even love's a weapon," R.P.W. comments).

It is R.P.W. who points out that, paradoxically, Lilburn had done all for love:

> For Love was all he asked, yet love
> Is the intolerable accusation of guilt
> To all the yearning Lilburns who cannot love,
> So must destroy who loves, and achieve at last
> The desiderated and ice-locked anguish of isolation.
>
> (113)

R.P.W.'s interpretation of the act is strikingly similar to the narrator-historian's analysis of Jeremiah Beaumont's motivation in *World Enough and Time*. Lilburn yearns toward "the peace of definition" and seeks that fulfillment in the "thrilling absoluteness of the pure act." His own motives are unsullied, for the murder of George was

> done for good,
> For his mother and the sweetness of the heart,
> And that's the instructive fact of history,
> That evil's done for good, and in good's name—
>
> (143)

Brother to Dragons moves toward its climax in the confrontation scene of Jefferson and his sister, Lucy. Jefferson, absolving himself of responsibility in the murder of George and condemning the immorality of his nephew's act, has concluded that the only reality is pain:

[124]

> We are born to joy that joy may become pain.
> We are born to hope that hope may become pain.
> We are born to love that love may become pain.
> We are born to pain that pain may become more
> Pain, and from that inexhaustible superflux
> We may give others pain as our prime definition—
>
> (131-32)

For Lucy, however, love not pain is the index of self-definition and the measure of man's humanity. Without condoning the act, she is ready to accept her share of the responsibility. Jefferson is deaf to Lucy's plea that he extend his hand to Lilburn in a gesture of the mutual responsibility and guilt that binds all humanity. At this moment in the action, Meriwether Lewis, Jefferson's "near-son" and spiritual heir, suddenly appears to charge Jefferson with betrayal. Inspired by Jefferson's noble view of man's innocence, Meriwether had gone out "to redeem the wild world far to the Western Shore" (37). Dazzled by the vision of man's goodness, Meriwether had been ill-equipped for the evil he encountered on the trail, and his disillusionment had driven him to suicide.

Shaken by the charge, Jefferson acknowledges his complicity in Meriwether's suicide. Lucy then leads her brother to the knowledge that his kinship with Lilburn is deeper than blood. Jefferson's vision of man's "natural innocence" and Lilburn's "whirling dream of desperate innocence" are both equally remote from a world in which good and evil are irremediably fused. Just as Lilburn had seen in George his "darkest self/And all the possibility of the dark that he feared," so Jefferson's repudiation of Lilburn had sprung from an unconscious dread that he too might be "capable of all." Accepting this knowledge of self, Jefferson can now accept the knowledge which Jack Burden had so painfully won from his excursion into the past: "The dream of the future is not/Better than the fact of the past, no matter how terrible./For without the fact of the past we cannot dream the future" (193).

It only remains for R.P.W. to ask the final question: "what is any knowledge/Without the intrinsic mediation of the heart?"

(212). Standing on the bluff near the ruins of Rocky Hill, he watches the river roll onward like an image of the sweep of history, but an image only. For nature is "but mirror to the human heart's steadfast and central illumination" (211), and it is man who superimposes meaning onto nature. Five years earlier, in 1946, R.P.W. had come to that bluff. There in the ruined garden he had confronted evil, symbolized by a great black snake, *elaphe obsoleta obsoleta*. In the course of his excursion into the past, he had observed, ironically, that the modern world is "advanced/Beyond the superstitious fear of God's wrath" (64). Evil, however, is not so obsolete as the snake's name might imply. Each man holds within himself the "rich detritus of all History" (122), the burden of past evil and the possibility of future good. Now, in 1951, having come to terms with the story of Lilburn Lewis, R.P.W. is ready to reaffirm what he affirmed on his first trip to the bluff—the necessity of virtue:

> The recognition of complicity is the beginning of innocence.
> The recognition of necessity is the beginning of freedom.
> The recognition of the direction of fulfillment is the death of
> the self.
> And the death of the self is the beginning of selfhood.
> All else is surrogate of hope and destitution of spirit.
>
> (214-15)

Then R.P.W. descends the mountain and, like Jack Burden at the close of *All the King's Men,* is ready to enter "the world of action and liability."

Upon its appearance in 1953, several reviewers called *Brother to Dragons* Warren's finest achievement and the best long narrative poem produced by an American in this century. The intervening decade since its publication has allowed the critical smoke to clear, but the passage of time has only served to confirm the early praise. In the novelty of its form, the freshness and flexibility of its idiom, and the narrative power of its blank verse, the poem seems to gain in stature and weight as the full measure of Warren's achievement becomes apparent. The poem clearly owes a debt to the earlier "Ballad of Billie Potts" in which Warren had alternated narrative and commentary, but in *Brother to Dragons* he has fused action and meaning in a way that carries the reader along on a rising wave of intellectual excitement.

Warren's great skill at characterization has never been more in evidence than in the pages of *Brother to Dragons.* Since his choice of a quasi-dramatic form meant the sacrifice of the usual expository and narrative devices for description and evocation of mood, the dialogue has to carry the entire burden of revealing character and forwarding action. Warren has managed to convey the unique flavor and slant of each character's speech while maintaining the unity of tone of the poem as a whole. The two women are particularly impressive. Lucy Lewis speaks with a firmly controlled eloquence which reflects her quiet dignity and lucid intelligence. Laetitia Lewis is less articulate, less profound; but her girlish and imploring appeals, couched in the vernacular of the frontier, are among the most touching passages in the poem. The same folk quality is carried over into the speech of Isham and of Laetitia's brother: the one, matter-of-fact and rooted in concrete experience; the other, bumptious and arrogant. Counterpointing the speech of these characters is the haunting and earthy Negro dialect of Aunt Cat. The speech of all the characters is unified by the pervasive imagery of light and dark, sun and shade (anticipated in the epigraph from Lucretius) which suggests, at one level, the polarities of knowledge and ignorance and, at another level, glory and damnation. Our lives must be worked out neither in the sunlit dazzle of innocence nor in the opaque darkness of malignant nature but "in the shade of the human condition" (193).

II

In 1955 Robert Penn Warren published *Band of Angels,* a novel which, like the two works that preceded it, was set in nineteenth-century Kentucky. But where *World Enough and Time* and *Brother to Dragons* had been greeted with enthusiasm and respect by the critics, *Band of Angels* was received with the cry that Warren had relaxed his standards. Here was a return to the unabashed historical romance, the Bosom Book, a pot-boiler tailored to the quick profits of the Hollywood market. The fact that a motion picture was soon made from the novel seemed to substantiate the criticism. Warren's very considerable narrative powers were at full stretch, and *Band of Angels,* the critics charged, was melodrama beyond the dreams of Margaret Mitchell.

"History," Warren has said, "is not melodrama, even if it usually reads like that."[13] If *Band of Angels* reads like melodrama, it is because of the novel's faithfulness to history. Warren has always had "a romantic kind of interest in the objects of American history: saddles, shoes, figures of speech";[14] and in *Band of Angels* he fully indulged that interest. Warren told Leonard Casper that he drew upon Winston Coleman's *Slavery Days in Kentucky* and Theodore Canot's *Adventures of an African Slaver,* as well as upon memoirs of officers on slave patrol, hearings in the British Parliament, and other documents from the Brown University and Yale University collections.[15] A great deal of attention has been lavished on the novel's interior decoration. Warren knows the heft of a Civil War rifle, the cut of a Yankee officer's coat, the look of a Baltimore clipper as it slips down the Patapsco River; and he renders them all with a kind of antiquarian zeal. At times there is such a clutter of detail, such an insistence on background authenticity, that the reader may feel—as does the visitor to some widely heralded Historical Restoration—that the scene has everything but the breath of life.

Such a criticism is not crucial in the case of *Band of Angels,* for Warren has evoked the past not for its own sake but for the way in which it at once reflects and illuminates his characters. And Warren can evoke the past. He understands, as he demonstrated in *World Enough and Time,* the ways of the historical imagination and energizes them with the novelist's art. *Band of Angels* draws on the epochal, incandescent events of American history in a way that *World Enough and Time* did not. John Brown strikes at Harper's Ferry, men die at Shiloh, the noose draws tighter about New Orleans, Farragut runs the forts.

The guns, however, boom faintly on the periphery of the novel, threatening but distant. The decisive public events are transmuted by Warren into symbols of personal histories. The conflicts that rage on the battlefield, the emancipation of the slaves, the horrors of Reconstruction—all have their counterparts in the soul of the novel's heroine, Amantha Starr. As she says early in the novel:

> You live through time, that little piece of time that is yours, but that piece of time is not only your own life, it is the summing-up of all the other lives that are simultaneous with yours. It is, in other words, History, and what you are is an expression of History, and you do not live your life, but somehow, your life lives you, and you are, therefore, only what History does to you."
>
> (112)

True, but only a partial truth, because as Amantha comes to see, "You are, also, what you do to History."

It is from the point of view of Amantha Starr, the daughter of a Kentucky planter and his Negro slave, that the reader sees the story. The opening sentences of the first two paragraphs state the central theme: first, Amantha's imploring question, "Oh, who am I?" followed by her cry, "if I could only be free." These are but a new set of terms for a working out of the by now familiar Warren problem, the problem of identity. Amantha is seeking to define herself or, as she puts it, "to make myself come true."

Amantha Starr is a singularly passive character, defined in large measure by the men who surround her. She tells her story with candor and modesty, but like those other—very different because more knowing—heroines of fiction Elizabeth Bennett and Becky Sharp, part of her charm is that she is desired by almost every man she meets. Amantha freely confesses acts of cowardice and disloyalty, disarmingly reveals that she knows the "sweet advantage of having been little and precious and wronged," yet her innocence and the pathos of her plight relieve her actions of any tinge of malice. As she enters into each new liaison, she gropes toward identity only to suffer again the "terror of abandonment."

Band of Angels opens with a memorable evocation of childhood, the first nine years of Amantha's life on a Kentucky plantation. These events are remembered "only in portentous disconnection, each in a kind of mystic isolation." The effect is that of leafing through a family album of daguerreotypes, the pictures blurred and faded with age, suspended out of time and place. This static, selective quality of memory carries over into adulthood. Amantha persists in remembering her life in snapshot glimpses frozen in memory until the shock of events causes her to see the past as a dynamic, shaping force in the present, for she wants her private history "to be fixed in the darkness of the past." She must learn that the darkness of the past is a "teeming darkness, straining soundlessly with forms struggling for recognition, for release from that dark realm of undifferentiated possibility" (218).

The crucial event remembered from Amantha's childhood is an episode with an old family retainer named Shadrach. While jouncing the child on his lap, Shadrach is told by her Mammy that Amantha is too old for such fondling. Trapped and enraged by the innuendo and aware that Amantha is the child of a mother who was neither white nor free, Shadrach pushes her contemptuously away, saying, "Yeah—what she?" When Amantha innocently relates the incident to her father, he summarily sells the old Negro, but not before Shadrach attempts to escape and is brutally beaten by his captors. Bewildered by the event, Amantha has the first hint of the "giddy insubstantiality" of childhood innocence. She is guiltily aware that she has somehow betrayed Shadrach's love and spat upon the "niggerness" in him. But as a legacy, Shadrach has left her with a question, "What she?" (13).

Amantha is taken to Cincinnati by her father where, under the tutelage of the sensuous and worldly Miss Idell, she is outfitted for Oberlin College. Miss Idell, foil to Amantha, plays gaily and successfully the roles of Mrs. Muller, Mrs. Starr, and Mrs. Morton. But she remains always in her own mind, as in the fancy of Amantha, Miss Idell. She is another of those secure and masterful Warren characters whose "certainty of self" is the despair and envy of the seekers for self-knowledge. In contrast to Miss Idell's confidence is Amantha's diffidence, embodied in the recurring images of dreaming and of the receding immensity of sky.

At Oberlin Amantha meets and falls in love with an ascetic theology student, Seth Parton; and from him she learns to mouth the pious clichés of Abolition—the argument from righteousness, the argument of self-interest. At Oberlin she also absorbs the pastoral vision of Negroes in their native Africa: "the sweet village where the flowers brilliantly bloomed and beloved faces lifted to greet them from the shadow of tiny bee-hive shaped grass huts" (62). Amantha, typically assuming the protective coloration of the environment into which she is thrust, is converted to Abolition and promptly challenges her father to free his slaves, oblivious to the irony that she is requiring of him her own freedom. Seeing his bumbling embarrassment in framing a reply, she feels "some hard sense of advantage just gained" (27). This tentative assertion of her identity—her new-found power over her father and the flattering attentions of Seth—vanishes with the crushing news that her father has died, an adulterer and, so rumor has it, an embezzler.

Returning to Kentucky to her father's funeral, Amantha is arrested by the sheriff at the grave to satisfy the claims made against her father's estate. Her father, torn between his guilt-ridden need to set free "little Manty" and his unwillingness to declare her less than his own child, had never drawn up the manumission papers. As a result, the terms of her self-definition are enlarged by two other men: the sheriff who gives her a legal definition, "female property," and the slave trader who gives her an economic one, "a nigger is what you can sell." She is thus reduced to chattel, a "non-person . . . suspended in the vacuum of no identity" (52). She proclaims her hatred of her father as, in the course of the novel, she proclaims, coldly and almost ritualistically, her hatred of each of the men in her life. Sold down the river like Shadrach, screaming and struggling, she sinks into a luxury she will continue to allow herself, the luxury of self-pity.

At New Orleans, Amantha is bought at auction by an aging cotton planter, Hamish Bond, whose name suggests both the biblical progenitor of the Negro race, Ham, and the ties that hold Amantha. Bond impulsively buys her, impelled in part by his urge to possess her and in part by a sense of pity. (He has, his former mulatto mistress remarks, "kindness like a disease.") Bond shares his creator's gift for language, and the account of his life—the familiar Warren pattern of a plot within a plot and a virtuoso display of his storytelling powers—is a harrowing version of the barbarism out of which the slaves came, a corrective to the idyllic picture of Africa that Amantha had learned at Oberlin.

Amantha's role in Bond's household is highly equivocal. He indulges her whims and makes no sexual demands upon her at first, but this illusory freedom only serves to accentuate the peculiar hold he has on her and the ambiguity of her racial composition. Legally a Negro, she can yet dream of an escape northward to "be lost in a world of white faces" (91). Amantha longs to have Bond decisively define her life, but he, like her father, cannot bring himself to free her for fear he will cease to possess her.

Amantha's life with Bond follows a pattern remarkably similar to her life at her father's plantation. In each instance, there is a terrifying storm which leads to a personal revelation, a plantation jubilee, and a romantic involvement. Each relationship is defined by an incident in which an older man leaps quixotically to the protection of a young girl, from which she gains "some hard secret sense of advantage" (135). In their cyclical pattern, these events emphasize Amantha's insistence on preserving inviolate her image of "Little Manty." Her own self-pity encourages her father and Bond to luxuriate in feelings of condescension toward her. The death of her father meant the end of the secure world of her childhood. As the Confederacy topples, her life with Hamish Bond collapses. Bond sets Amantha "free" in war-torn New Orleans only to return after the city is under martial law to ask her to marry him. By this time, however, she is engaged to marry one of the "liberators," a Union officer named Tobias Sears.

Amantha's problem is, as Leslie Fiedler has pointed out, that she cannot will to say the words, "I am a Negro."[16] This admission is impossible for her, for such an avowal would turn her life into something to be lived instead of something to be deplored. The tension in Amantha's mind concerning her race is developed and controlled by Warren's varied and complex handling of the black-white imagery. The connotations which cluster about the poles of black and white—primitivism and civilization, slavery and freedom, ignorance and knowledge—indicate the direction of Amantha's pilgrimage. The reader is constantly aware that the action is unfolding against the dazzling white of the cotton fields with the ominous blackness of the forests as a back drop. At her father's funeral, Amantha is struck by "the ladies in black, . . . the faces white and staring at me," a memory that returns to haunt her. There is the Dantesque scene of a Negro being prepared for the slave market in a tub of scalding water, "the vapor wreathing up whitely about his black skinniness." And in her despair Amantha cries, when offered a lamp by a servant, "For me, it's all the same! Light or dark" (78).

This black-white polarity is maintained, with diagrammatic exactness, in the contrast of Hamish Bond's two associates who desire Amantha, Rau-Ru and Charles Prieur-Denis. Rau-Ru is the *K'la*, a favored overseer at Bond's upriver plantation and a kind of secret sharer or alter ego. When Amantha first sees him, she is struck by the "face of preternatural blackness, like enameled steel, against the white of the loose blouse." Although Rau-Ru achieves his own freedom, Amantha associates him with the world of slavery from which she would gladly escape. Set off against Rau-Ru is Charles Prieur-Denis, "a figure in white trousers and black coat of silky sheen." His elegant and exotic manner disguises a sharper, swindler and slave-runner who would use Bond's plantation for a barracoon. Bond, "to test his weakness," perversely throws his "pore little Manty" and Charles together, but Charles's attempt at a seduction is thwarted by

Rau-Ru. Charles is gravely injured in the resulting fracas, and Rau-Ru, denied a hearing in court because of his color, flees to the forest. As these men destroy themselves for her, Amantha remains aloof, singularly passive and uncomprehending: "I was thinking of my own suffering, my disarray of spirit, my disorientation and fear."

The concluding section of the novel takes as its theme Amantha's effort to find identity through her marriage to Tobias Sears. Sears, an Emersonian of the Brahmin stamp, is yet another of the familiar Warren clan of uncompromising idealists which includes Percy Munn, Adam Stanton, and Jeremiah Beaumont. He speaks mistily of his devotion to the "idea" beyond the realities of this world. He has, Amantha says, "nobility like a disease."

Determined to devote his life to the cause of freeing the slaves, he insists on a Negro command during the Civil War, a "real blue-gum commission," and after Appomattox accepts a post in the Freedman's Bureau. Like Jack Burden, Tobias loves Truth, but his truth has a way of being the obverse of the truth of those he suspects of having influence over him. With Tobias, Amantha hopes to "start life over, to make our world of loving kindness." Her decision is a renewed affirmation of identity founded on the denial of her personal history. She will cancel the past with a resolution.

But Tobias fails—"failing westward" in Amantha's phrase—infected by the materialism of Reconstruction which attracts him even while it repels him. Nor is he able to reconcile the idealism of his great crusade for Negro rights with the reality of a wife whose mother was a slave. Such insight into self as he is granted comes while engaged in the serio-comic reclamation of the Negro garbage collector of Halesburg, Kansas. It is only when Tobias sees himself reflected in the pitying and contemptuous glance of a rich Negro from Chicago—sees himself, that is, not as "the bearer of freedom" of his imagination but as the drunkard and failure that he is—can he affirm the brotherhood of the dispossessed. In a moment of illumination, he discovers he had deluded himself and demeaned his wife. With

Tobias' abdication of his role as "liberator," Amantha can now proclaim her own emancipation; for she has discovered that dependence is a trap and "nobody can set you free . . . except yourself" (303). "Don't ever call me little Manty again," she tells Tobias and, at a stroke, discards the protective, self-pitying image which has been the prop of a lifetime, and enters into the "awfulness of joy."

The cast of characters is so varied and so fully-realized in *Band of Angels* and the narrative so vivid and powerful that it is difficult to account for the fact that the final impression the novel leaves is unsatisfactory. John M. Bradbury is certainly correct when he complains of the flat and anticlimactic ending.[17] The "joy" which cancels the "old shadows" is unconvincing, for Amantha's ultimate illumination lacks the conviction of the struggles which have led up to it. Amantha herself is not so persuasive as other Warren *raisonneurs*. We are asked to believe in the essential passivity of her character even when it seems strongly at variance with the speculative bent of her mind. It strains credibility to believe that a character so reflective can at the same time be so insensitive. Consequently, the ideas with which Warren is concerned seem remote from the events which embody them. The richness of the experience is so memorably expressed that the ideas seem attenuated and super-imposed upon the narrative.

Perhaps *Band of Angels* is finally the victim of its place in the Warren canon. After the success of *All the King's Men,* Warren devoted a decade to exploring the historical materials of his native Kentucky. *World Enough and Time* is a major achievement and illustrates Delmore Schwartz's insight that Warren's fiction seems often to aspire to the condition of narrative poetry.[18] After a decade of poetic silence, Warren's poetic, dramatic and narrative gifts were superbly fused in *Brother to Dragons,* and the triumph of this tale in verse and voices naturally had raised expectations concerning his next work. *Band of Angels,* although an eminently readable novel, can only pale in comparison to its distinguished predecessors.

CHAPTER *6*

Interim Report

IN AN INTERVIEW for the *Paris Review* in 1957, Robert Penn Warren acknowledged a change during the preceding decade in his "personal relation" toward his writing. "I quit writing poems for several years," he said. "I'd start them, get a lot down, then feel that I wasn't connecting somehow. I didn't finish one for several years, they felt false. Then I got back at it, and that is the bulk of what I've done since *Band of Angels* —a new book of poems."[1] This new volume, *Promises, Poems 1954-1956*, was the first book of lyric poetry Warren had published since *Selected Poems*, thirteen years earlier. More warmly received than any book Warren had written since *All the King's Men*, *Promises* won the Pulitzer Prize and the National Book Award.

Like Warren's earlier poetry, the poems in *Promises* are written in a variety of verse forms—sonnets, lullabies, lyrics, and, in "Dragon Country," even a variation on the tall tale of the frontier. These poems manifest the same wide technical resources and speak with the same fierce honesty as Warren's earlier verse. His clear-eyed recognition of "our time's sad declension" is still evident, as is his acute sense of disillusionment, his insistence that human nature is fundamentally perverse and endlessly paradoxical. But the volume has its surprises. *Promises*, as its title suggests, speaks quietly of a "sunlit chance" and a "dawning perspective and possibility of human good." The lines are vibrant with a warmth at variance with the crabbed intellectuality of some of Warren's earlier poetry. This is not to say that *Promises* is flaccid in either thought or phrase. Offering neither easy consolation nor glib evasion, these poems are a mature recognition of the terror of the human condition and a sense of the possibility of ultimate triumph over it. The recognition springs from an apprehension of the "necessity of truth," and the possibility of triumph from the knowledge that "there's natural distress/In learning to face Truth's glare-glory."

These insights are couched in a form which, in contrast to the scoured, burnished verses of the earlier poetry, has a greater ease of movement and a more varied rhythm. The cold perfection of some of Warren's earlier poetry is replaced by a studied roughening. Having demonstrated his mastery of traditional forms, Warren has tried to go beyond them at the risk of being charged with ineptitude and cacophony. In reaching out for new effects, he may have had in mind a quality he noted in Melville's poetry: "Perhaps the violences, the distortions, the wrenchings in the versification of some of the poems are to be interpreted as . . . a conscious effort to develop a nervous, dramatic, masculine style."[2]

Promises is distinctly personal in tone and subject, and in this respect the volume follows the direction already foreshadowed in *Brother to Dragons*. Even though Warren's almost compulsive concern with certain plot situations and character types betokens a source in his personal experience, he had always fully assimilated the materials and subordinated them to his intention. In *Promises*, however, Warren seems impelled to exploit the materials of his experience directly. The personal note is struck immediately in the dedications to the two sections of the volume: the first to Warren's daughter, Rosanna, "a little girl, one year old, in a ruined fortress," and the second to his son, Gabriel.

The sequence of five poems to Rosanna which opens the volume is set on a stretch of Italian seashore north of Rome where Warren and his wife have taken their daughter. The first three poems, written in a loose variation of the sonnet form, describe a sun-drenched landscape of vineyards sweeping down to a sand beach sheltered from the waves by black lava-chunks. On a seacliff overlooking the Mediterranean, a fortress, once the symbol of a Spanish monarch's power, is now reduced to a rubble of stones overgrown with golden gorse and thistle. Near the fortress lives the *gobbo*—the hunchback—with his sullen, glaring wife. Seven of their children play in the dirt outside the house; the eighth is defective, the result of the mother's unsuccessful attempt at abortion. About the scene is the aura of an old and spent civilization, the sense of time and history stretching endlessly backward. The "classic pose" of an engaged couple, the "triptych beauty" of the *gobbo*'s little girl who is "beautiful like a saint," and the predominate tones of gold and blue remind us of a magnificent Italian past in contrast to the ugliness of the present—garbage in the moat, the "monster" child next door. Against this background of an incredibly ancient and "ruined world" is the laughing and golden-haired Rosanna, innocent and vulnerable, a symbol of promise and renewal.

"The Flower," the fourth and finest poem of the series, is a little parable that embodies the controlling idea of the volume—the promise, a covenant between the generations that will be abrogated or fulfilled. Each day at twilight as the poet, his wife, and their daughter climb from the beach to the hill fortress, they come to a favorite spot in the path where the child always demands a white flower to carry in her hand. The parents share her childlike delight in the ritual, and in token of their own happiness, the mother every afternoon since early June has put a blue flower in the child's yellow hair. As the season wanes, the flowers fade, and inevitably the day arrives when there is no bloom "worthily white." But the little girl still insists on even a "ruined" flower and sings "as though human need/ Were not for perfection." The poet, musing on the child's joyous acceptance, can suspend for a moment his adult fears of a multiform world of flux and change and, in the simple innocence of the scene before him, can proclaim the oneness of human life:

> And in that image let
> Both past and future forget,
> In clasped communal ease,
> Their brute identities.

As he ascends the hill, the poet looks back once more toward the bay and watches a white gull turn suddenly black against the sunset, then circle back toward the east. The poet follows the arc of the bird's flight and, in the moment before it dips below the mountain, sees it gleam suddenly and hopefully white in the last light. As darkness falls, the poet and child hear the familiar rustling of the surf with its promise of a new dawn.

Among the series of poems dedicated to Gabriel are several which have Italian settings linking them to the Rosanna sequence, but in general the poems to Gabriel are grounded in the South of Warren's youth. In "Hands Are Paid," for example, the speaker recalls a single working day in the life of a farmhand. The scene, evidently Warren's boyhood Kentucky, returns to him in all its specificity: sweat-cold overalls, a mule's head at the barn-lot bar, the clatter of a red thresher. The farmhand comes home exhausted, eats his sowbelly and cornbread, kicks off his shoes, and falls heavily into bed. Remembering the scene on a "foreign shore," the speaker names over each item "but cannot think/What, in their urgency, they must mean." The Gabriel sequence constitutes an effort to determine that meaning.

The search for the meaning of the past is nothing new in Warren, but the renewed urgency of his quest springs from the need to define the world of his youth not only to his own satisfaction but to that of his son. Ranging backward to encompass Warren's parents, as well as the Southern heritage in its broader reaches, these poems, in their personal aspects, constitute a legacy to Gabriel from all who have gone before. In the opening poem, "What Was the Promise That Smiled from the Maples at Evening?" the poet's father, Robert Franklin Warren, speaks from the grave to all succeeding generations: "We died only that every promise might be fulfilled." In "Founding Fathers, Nineteenth Century Style, Southeast U.S.A.," a marvelously distilled interpretation of the Southern tradition, the names made familiar by the textbooks—Sam Houston, James Bowie, Henry Clay—speak across the years, as do others unknown to fame. Among them are two of Warren's own ancestors, a land shark "not well trusted" and a crusty old veteran of Shiloh.

They offer no advice for our "complexity of choices,/But beg us only one word to justify their own old life-cost."

> So let us bend ear to them in this hour of lateness,
> And what they are trying to say, try to understand,
> And try to forgive them their defects, even their greatness,
> For we are their children in the light of humanness, and under
>   the shadow of God's closing hand.

Among the most memorable poems in *Promises* are the verse narratives. These poems might have been cast as short stories twenty years earlier, but Warren declared in 1959 that he would write no more short fiction. "Poems," he said at that time, "are great devourers of short stories."[3] Both "School Lesson" and "Country Burying (1919)" are typical Warren short stories distilled into verse. At least two poems, "Court-martial" and "Dark Night of," are superb retellings of earlier stories, themselves among Warren's best.

"Dark Night of" is a return to the experience already realized in "Blackberry Winter." A twelve-year-old boy, bookish, curious, innocent, sees an old and grizzled tramp lurking in the forest bordering his father's farm. Going to fetch the cows, the boy comes suddenly upon the tramp who is lying exhausted in a clump of honeysuckle. Their eyes "thread the single thread/Of the human entrapment" until the tramp pitifully begs the boy to get away. But since the child, entranced by the pathos of the tramp's condition, cannot tear his eyes away, the old man stumbles to his feet and continues his journey which "no man would have planned." In contrast to "Blackberry Winter," "Dark Night of" grants the moment of illumination not to the boy but to the tramp. Having experienced the "absolute and glacial purity of despair," the tramp is able to enter into the "awfulness of joy."

"Court-martial" delineates the relationship of a boy and his grandfather that is not unlike the one Warren explored in his story "When the Light Gets Green." The poem is concerned with the boy's efforts to "untie/The knot of History." Under the eyes of the old captain of cavalry, the child with his toy soldiers fights again the campaigns of the Civil War, certain that "death is only the glory." A chance question elicits from the old man a brutal tale of court-martialing guerrillas. "Two lieutenants talk law," and then, without mercy or compunction, the guerrillas were taken to the woods and hanged. The rapt, horrified stare of the little boy at the disclosure wrings from the old man an involuntary cry of conscience. In the "darkening air" the child's unblemished image of his grandfather is shattered, and the boy realizes that he, in his innocence, has passed judgment on his grandfather's guilt.

Warren's theme of the evanescence of the past is restated in one of the loveliest lyrics in *Promises,* "Walk by Moonlight in Small Town." The speaker of the poem, like so many Warren characters, has come back to his home town—"every ticket's round trip." The little town, smaller even than remembered, stands pitiful and ugly; but the moonlight transforms it into a place of eerie beauty. Each street and building holds some memory, some scrap of the past; and the poet yearns to know their meaning, to realize an ideal forever beyond the human world of imperfection:

Might a man but know his Truth, and might
He live so that life, by moon or sun,
In dusk or dawn, would be all one,
Then never on a summer night
Need he stand and shake in that cold blaze of Platonic light.

I

Promises was followed in 1960 by *You, Emperors, and Others, Poems 1957-1960* which is linked to the earlier volume in both theme and form. The lyric "Debate: Question, Quarry, Dream" recalls the Gabriel sequence, speaking as it does of an infant son and his father's "appalling logic of joy." The satiric, slangy idiom of "Nocturne" and "Man in the Street" relates them to "Ballad of a Sweet Dream of Peace" in *Promises,* as well as to the novel Warren was writing simultaneously, *The Cave.* Although *You, Emperors* lacks the thematic unity of *Promises,* the later volume offers a wider variety of formal effects. In addition to lullabies and verse narratives, there are parodies of nursery rhymes, epigrams, an elegy, and a ballad.

You, Emperors takes its title from the two groups of poems which open the volume. In the first, an eight-poem series entitled "Garland for You," the central concern is the search for definition: the need "To recognize/The human self naked in your own eyes." The *you* of the poems is everyman, the face staring back from the mirror that one cannot meet or, meeting, cannot recognize. The poem may address the man in the "Ivy League flannel suit," "Mr. and Mrs. North and South America," or, as in the second series entitled "Two Pieces after Suetonius," the emperors Domitian and Tiberius. It is apparent, however, that, as the opening poem declares, "Whoever you are, this poem is clearly about you."

Among the poems that make up "Garland for You" is "The Letter about Money, Love, or Other Comfort, If Any," a splendid example of compressed narrative and inventive language. The metrics of this poem indicate something of the combination of strictness and freedom found in Warren's later poetry. "The Letter," one long sentence, is composed of eight stanzas each of eleven lines of varying length. Although no rhythmic pattern clearly emerges, there is a complex and scrupulously observed rhyme scheme, ABBACDCDEDE.

As the narrator of the poem reaches his doorstep one moon-lit night, a sinister stranger materializes from the shrubbery, thrusts a letter at him, laughs balefully, and vanishes. The speaker, filled with youthful innocence and possessed of a "passion, like a disease, for Truth," undertakes to deliver the letter "By Hand Only." This trust, it turns out, is the work of a lifetime and is, distressingly, a "metaphysical runaround." The trail leads from Nashville and Dubuque to New England, abroad to Rome and Paris, then back to San Francisco. He hears at last that his quarry has fled to a high mountain shelf, and there the speaker resolves to leave the letter under a cairn marked with a red bandanna.

This bizarre quest is, it becomes clear, a means of coming to terms with the deepest self. For the "you" addressed in the poem turns out to be an elusive Other Self with whom the speaker, although always a step behind, must compulsively keep pace. Restlessly seeking his own truth, the Other Self has tried membership in the Episcopal Church, rustication in New England, suicide in Italy, casual sin in Paris. About him there is something irrational and subhuman. Having left a trail of squalor and violence, he finally sinks into nature and, the speaker has heard, has become "capable of all bestiality." After tracking his quarry this far, the speaker, now aged and infirm, announces that he will abandon his effort to confront the Other Self and will leave the letter and his "obligation" on the mountain. Descending in the blaze of dawn, he will "seek/the way, and my peace with God." But the resolution has a hollow ring, for the speaker's salvation seems somehow dependent on his keeping faith with this darker self.

The third series of *You, Emperors*, "Mortmain," is a cycle of five poems dealing with the poet's father. This series is, Warren has said, "clearly personal. Further, the personal urgencies are dramatized, are overtly presented, not merely absorbed."[4] "Mortmain" represents still another variation on the theme of the poems to Gabriel in *Promises*. In that sequence the birth of his son has led the poet to examine his childhood. In "Mortmain" the death of his father forces upon him a re-examination of the past and its meaning. The memories of his father's youth with its early promise and inevitable disappointments are rendered more poignant by the poet's small son who, surrounded by a teddy bear and letter blocks, laughs from a farther room. "I/Do not want to weep," the poet says, "I want to understand."

The title of the opening poem of "Mortmain" speaks with the blunt insistence of a newspaper headline: "After Night Flight Son Reaches Bedside of Already Unconscious Father, Whose Right Hand Lifts in a Spasmodic Gesture, As Though Trying to Make Contact: 1955." The poem opens with a series of images all pointing to the idea of order. The poet has rushed by plane in "Time's concatenation" across the "abstract flight-grid of sky." Arriving at the bedside, he watches his father's waxy hand claw up "like law" from the "ritualistically reordered" covers. In contrast to these images of pattern and order are the hysterical disconnections of the poet's mind:

> . . . *oh, oop-si-daisy,* churns
> The sad heart, *oh, atta-boy, daddio's got*
> *One more shot in the locker, peas-porridge hot—*

Through such abrupt shifts in tone, Warren communicates the intense strain of attempting to hold in check a mind plunged into deep grief, a technique which recalls an earlier poem on the same theme, "The Return: An Elegy." In a single gesture of recognition and loss, the relationship of father and son is brought sharply into focus. The feeble hand of the father holds within it the son's own life, and the son's affirmation of selfhood—the "I" which the meter of the poem continually thrusts at the reader—is negated by the father's gesture, leaving the son "Naked in that black blast of his love."

In the concluding poem of the "Mortmain" series, the poet has a vision of his father as a young boy in Trigg County, Kentucky. The poet, in the autumn of his life, looks down the "tube and darkening corridor of Time" and sees the youth "poised between woods and the pasture, sun-green and green shadow." Aware of what time holds in store for his father, the poet yearns to speak across the years: "Out of my knowledge, I would cry out and say:/*Listen!* Say: *Listen! I know—Oh I know—let me tell you!*" But the "hieratic" boy turns "with imperial calm" and re-enters the shadow of the woods, confident of his own springtime promise.

"Two Studies in Idealism: Short Survey of American, and Human, History" are dramatic monologues spoken, apparently from Valhalla, by two soldiers killed in the Civil War. By contrasting two psychological types, the poems explore the unspoken and only half-understood human needs which prompt men to selfless, heroic conduct. In "Bear Track Plantation" a Confederate soldier, although a man of coarse and uncomplicated sensuality, longs for "something to save from the mess" of life and to "know what he lives for." The Yankee in "Harvard '61:

Battle Fatigue" is more complex. He is confident that he has proved his manhood "by dying for Right," but he is disturbed and even vexed by the men who died for reasons less exalted, who "parody with their own dying that Death which only Right should sustain." In the midst of the slaughter the young Harvard graduate had striven to keep his heart pure, and he is satisfied that he killed "without rancor." He assures us that he is "glad to be dead" and beyond "life's awful illogic," but he is still irked by the others, like the grizzled and profane veteran of "Bear Track Plantation," who died "with ghastly impertinence." The ironic treatment of these characters suggests how deeply rooted is the idealistic impulse in our nature and what contorted forms it can take. These poems look forward to Warren's treatment of still another variety of idealism against a Civil War background in his latest novel, *Wilderness.*

The energy and originality of *Promises* and *You, Emperors* bode well for Warren's future poetic development. Having established his reputation with a flexible and highly personal style, Warren has not been content merely to produce facile imitations of his early work. On the contrary, he has been quite willing to risk failure. When these later poems fail, and a number of them do, they fail by stating their themes abstractly and stridently. An example is the closing stanza of "He Has Fled" in *You, Emperors* which proclaims its theme so blatantly as to seem almost a self-parody. Warren's best poems, however, dramatize human experience in all its richness and complexity. As Cleanth Brooks has said, Warren's poetry "is hard to summarize, not because of its vagueness but because of its precision. 'What it says'—the total experience, which includes the speaker's attitude as part of it—the total experience can be conveyed by no document less than the poem itself."[5]

II

Warren's two most recent novels sustain the note of affirmation sounded in his latest volumes of poetry, and the novels, like the poems, represent a radical departure in form from the work that preceded them. The first of these novels, *The Cave*, published in 1959, had its genesis in an actual historical event. In January, 1925, Warren, then a senior at Vanderbilt, watched with the rest of the country the tragedy of Floyd Collins trapped in nearby Sand Cave, Kentucky. Young Collins was exploring an underground passage near Mammoth Cave in search of something to attract tourists when a large stone became dislodged, pinning his foot. An enterprising reporter for a Louisville newspaper slithered through the slime to interview Collins. The reports from the scene caught the national fancy, and a barrage of headlines and bulletins kept the public in a state of suspense concerning Collins' plight. Within two weeks a tent city had sprung up near the cave mouth, and milling crowds had to be restrained by state troopers with drawn bayonets. Since Collins could not be reached through the cave passage, an effort was made to cut a shaft from outside. When on the eighteenth day he was found dead, his body was sealed in the cave and funeral services were held on the hill above. This event provided a dramatic instance of the power of the mass media to stir the populace by an assault on their emotions. Within a month a North Carolina cave-in caught seventy-one men and fifty-three were killed. "It attracted," Frederick Lewis Allen observed drily, "no great notice."[6]

Collins' death was of "no great importance," Allen added; and it is the irony of such a statement that would attract Warren. Jereboam Beauchamp was, after all, a man "of no historical importance," as was the fictional Cass Mastern and the Roman citizen who supplies the epigraph for "Clearly About You." For Warren, the interest lies in the human significance of the situation and the meaning inherent in it. *The Cave* centers on an incident similar to the Collins story. (The actual story of Collins is alluded to once in the narrative as an earlier parallel.) The time of the novel is the spring of 1955, and the place is a world already explored in *At Heaven's Gate*: a large Southern city and a small rural town in Tennessee. The action traces three days in the life of Johntown—the involvement of a dozen or so townsfolk in the suffering of a "cave-crawler,"

Jasper Harrick, and the crass and cynical exploitation of that suffering by the "Big Media."

After his experiments with multiple frames of reference in *All the King's Men* and *World Enough and Time* and the straightforward first-person narration of *Band of Angels,* Warren controls and formalizes his materials in *The Cave* by employing a shifting angle of vision which reduces the need for authorial commentary. The action rendered symbolically is itself an interpretation. The central event of the novel, a young man trapped in a cave, is refracted through the consciousness of each of a group of very limited and imperfect human beings: people trapped by their narrowness of self, who convey their perceptions and sensations in a language suited to their backgrounds and experience. The variety of voices made possible a broad range of styles and released Warren's gift for earthy and often ribald humor which had been seldom in evidence since *All the King's Men.*

The characters of *The Cave* have, in several instances, the familiarity of people already encountered in Warren's fiction. Jack Harrick, "old heller of high coves and hoot-owl hollows," like Sergeant Alvin York of Pall Mall, Tennessee, is a country blacksmith who won the Congressional Medal of Honor in France. Although Warren had already drawn such a figure in Private Porsum of *At Heaven's Gate,* he makes Harrick an older Porsum, more fully realized than the dim and insubstantial character of the earlier work. Like Porsum, Harrick is a hillbilly, extraordinarily gifted with a rifle and a "slight for cover," but is first baffled and then victimized by his heroism and its consequences. Betrayed by an overweening faith in his physical vitality, he is dying of cancer and can find small spiritual comfort from his conversion to Christianity. Jack's son Jasper is also a war hero, having distinguished himself in Korea. He is another familiar figure in the Warren canon—Captain Todd in *Night Rider* is an example, as is Miss Idell of *Band of Angels—* a person blessed with a certainty of self which is the envy and despair of those around them: "He had that trick of being himself so completely, it looked like he wore the whole world over his shoulders like a coat" (19). The source of Jasper's confidence remains a mystery, for he is the only major character into whose consciousness we do not enter.

Jack Harrick's boyhood friend, the Reverend MacCarland Sumpter, is a kind of first cousin to the Scholarly Attorney in *All the King's Men*. Each, having faced the agonizing truth that his wife has carried the child of another man, sublimates that knowledge into a dogged, fanatic faith. Both are driven by the fear that their faith may prove under stress to be built on sand. Each has reared a boy whom he believes to be cynical and irreverent. Sumpter's son, Isaac, shares with Jack Burden a rather sophomoric cynicism and a wise-cracking style compounded of slang and profanity interlarded with literary allusions. There is something, too, of Jerry Calhoun in Isaac Sumpter, for both have about them the smell of success, both are untroubled by self-knowledge, and both are lost.

To point up these similarities to earlier characters is not to suggest a weakening in Warren's creative powers or a descent into redundancy but to insist on the consistency of the line of his artistic development and the integrity with which he has returned again and again to plumb more deeply certain characteristic themes and situations. As a matter of fact, the novel contains a gallery of diverse and freshly observed characters. One of these is "the Greek," Nicholas Papadoupalous, for whom Johntown is the latest in a list of failures southward: Cincinnati, Louisville, Nashville. Nick—physically powerful, suspicious, unlucky, and stupid—impetuously marries a dancer in a burlesque show because she reminds him of Jean Harlow, the movie queen of the 1930's. Now, however, she is slowly and expensively dying of tuberculosis, and Nick is deeply in debt to the Johntown bank. Its president, Timothy Bingham—cowardly, self-doubting, ineffectual—represents together with his wife, Matilda, the gentility of Johntown. Their marriage, a misalliance, reaches its crisis with the discovery that their only daughter, Jo-Lea, is pregnant with the child of Jack Harrick's younger son, Monty.

The novel's epigraph, drawn from the Allegory of the Cave, gives us the first clue to its meaning. The story, one of the most famous passages in Plato's *Republic,* is deservedly known. The inhabitants of a cave have been obliged to live out their lives chained with their backs to the mouth of the cave, unable to see the light of truth burning above and behind them. Knowing only the shadows cast on the wall at the rear of the cave and mistaking the echoes from the wall for the source of the sounds they hear, they accept the shadowy illusion for the reality they cannot know. Even if they were unshackled from their chains and forced to contemplate the light, they would find it distressing and painful. Only by being dragged reluctantly to the mouth of the cave could they be persuaded that their familiar world of shadows is not real and that the brilliant light outside is not merely a brighter illusion. It is just such a cave that Warren shows us in his novel. Each character is committed to his own version of a shadow world and, in being compelled by circumstances to face reality, each must leave the dark cavern of his own nature to face the light of self-knowledge. For Isaac Sumpter, the knowledge of self is too painful to accept, and he clings to the familiar illusory world. For others, emergence is a kind of rebirth, a recognition and acceptance of the essential self.

Warren has adapted Plato's basic metaphor and used it with countless variations for his own purposes. Characters are repeatedly shown in deep shadow, squinting into the brilliance outside and failing to grasp the implications of what they see. An example is the idle speculations of Jack Harrick's wife, Celia: "She kept . . . looking out from the shadow of the hall, then out under the deepening shadow of the maple boughs in the yard and the big cedars, out into the open where the light lay so sweet and far away like a place she would never come again" (290). Again, at the climax of the novel: "Jack Harrick had to force himself to face the open door, where the shadows of the hall piled up. Then he saw the figure appear in the space. The face, white against the shadows, was the face of MacCarland Sumpter" (377).

The patterns of imagery of the novel reinforce and elaborate the symbolism of the cave. Jack Harrick, troubled by a vague disquietude, contemplates the "big black hole right in the middle of him where a man's thinking and feeling and living ought to be" (139). When he meets the woman he will marry, Celia Hornby, he tells her: "I bet if I threw a rock down your well, I'd be listening down in the dark a long time before it hit water" (168). Monty Harrick, in the early days of his courtship of Jo-Lea Bingham, had not allowed her "to enter the darkened room of his fantasy" (8). Nicholas Papadoupalous broods on his repeated failures "in the deep, dark, angry, tear-sodden secret center of his being" (41). MacCarland Sumpter, lamenting his wife's death in childbirth, felt "as though a level of black water rose from the floor to overwhelm him" (83). Finally, the cave symbolism of the novel merges in the mind of Sumpter's son, Isaac, for in the cave in which Jasper is trapped, he sees an emblem of the mystery of his own personality:

> Maybe he would go into that cave and not come out. He shut his eyes and he heard the cold, deep sound of water from the pit in the cave, in the fourth chamber. In the absolute darkness of his head—and the pit—he saw a body in the absolute darkness of the roiling water, and even wondered how he could see it, in absolute darkness.
>
> Whether it was his own body, or Jasper Harrick's, he couldn't tell. No, it was not Jasper's, it had to be his own, for if you couldn't see anything, you could still feel things, and if he knew that the body was there, it would have to be because he himself was the body in that water, and he himself was that knowledge in that absolute darkness.
>
> (193)

The shadow of Sigmund Freud falls across the novel, for the cave symbolism has the particular connotations of womb and tomb which Freudian theory has taught us to attach to it. The cave is, literally, the tomb of Jasper Harrick; and Isaac Sumpter is overcome with inexorable envy for him "because he lay in the cool, cool dark and did not suffer" (324). Warren depicts the consequences of the longing for withdrawal and non-being in nightmare images of claustrophobic terror. Isaac Sumpter, fearful that his privacy has been breached, feels a "sudden terror at being spied on, as though he were spinning

away, down and down, into the depths of an astronomical tele-
scope" (104). And then there is the cry of Miss Abernathy,
confessing publicly that she has sinned carnally with Jack
Harrick: "It was a thin, wailing cry of lostness, like somebody falling down a well, a well infinitely deep" (321).

The cave is, also, a womb-like retreat where Jasper can "lie
snug and complete with the whole world tucked in around
him" (19). The cave as womb symbol functions on another level
as an aspect of the theme of rebirth. Isaac Sumpter, entering
the cave to search for Jasper, senses a new confidence stirring
within himself and formulates this feeling in imagery reminiscent
of the rebirth motif in *All the King's Men*:

> . . . his self was the self that knew that this being now stirred
> in the dew-darkness. But it had to be a self, for it was contained
> in the darkness which was himself. It was, he knew in a knowl-
> edge that was not quite knowledge, at least not quite words, a
> self of the self, a free, immortal self, ready for song, being born
> this instant in the darkness of the self that suffered and was free.
> (99)

Related to the concept of the cave as womb symbol is Warren's
reliance on sexual motivation in the delineation of character.
He has given us an exhaustive and explicit account of the sex
lives of the people of Johntown. There are the fantasies of
Nicholas Papadoupalous, the deprivations of Timothy Bingham,
and the "absoluteness and animality" of Isaac Sumpter. Jack
Harrick catalogues his epic fornications in the closing pages of
the novel until it seems a man's life consists in the number of
women he possesses. What gives these scenes of sexuality their
particular horror is not so much the coarse language in which
they are described, although it is tasteless to a degree, as the
lack of any degree of human warmth in them. Sex is either a
form of coldly egotistical aggression or a violent and mechanical
coupling. The cave of sexuality, like the cave of illusion,.
reverberates hollowly.

Ironically, these people are using sex as a proclamation of self.
Crippled emotionally by blunted sensibilities and plodding

minds, they are nevertheless groping confusedly in the shadows, searching for some light of truth, and as usual in Warren's work, the search for truth begins with the search for identity. To dramatize the blurring of identity in his characters, Warren has elaborated a technique he has used before: the multiplying of names for his characters to suggest the variety of masks with which they face the world. Jack Harrick is "Jumping Jack" to his buddies in the United States Army, a sexual athlete and a slaughterer of the Hun. To his wife, twenty-five years his junior, he is "John T.," for she finds in his masculinity a symbol of dominance she never found in her father. To the hillbillies, he is "Old Jack," an almost mythic figure. Isaac Sumpter, when living parasitically with a wealthy co-ed at the university, Rachel Goldstein, nicknames her, significantly enough, "Goldie." Later, when she is only a projection of his own self-esteem, she is simply generalized into the "Jew Girl." His own shifting sense of identity is betrayed when, in signing either his love letters or his by-line for the press, he hesitates craftily between "Isaac" and "Ikey." Nicholas Papadoupalous, estranged by his foreignness in xenophobic Johntown, cannot find a single citizen in the county who can pronounce his name correctly. His wife, Sarah Pumfret, has taken the stage name of Giselle Fontaine, but to her husband she is, at least in fantasy, Jean Harlow.

The Cave is a story of communal guilt, for, as MacCarland Sumpter points out, Jasper Harrick is re-enacting the plight of each man trapped in the darkness which is himself. Every man is diminished by the death of Jasper, and this ebbing of vitality is symbolized in the novel by the recurring image of bleeding. Nicholas Papadoupalous, his world slipping out of control, "felt like he was bleeding away in weakness" (267). Celia Harrick feels a sense of defraudment, "like a tiny wound bleeding its single silky thread of blood on her white skin" (294). Isaac Sumpter's vague stirrings of discontent are "like a tiny ulcer in his brain, unhealing forever and oozing" (366).

These examples, only a few of the many possible, suggest the symbolic richness that gives *The Cave* a texture unlike anything else in Warren's fiction. At times, however, the very profusion of imagery seems a mechanical and calculated intrusion rather than an integral part of the action. The conclusion of the novel, a series of Joycean epiphanies in which the central characters achieve a measure of serenity and self-knowledge, seems forced and gratuitous. Jack Harrick's final insight—"I reckon living is just learning how to die. And . . . dying [is] just learning how to live"—comes with the thud of anticlimax. As a study of limited and very human people who find themselves inadequate to the demands of a complex and value-stripped society, *The Cave* is a solid, moving performance. As a study of rebirth and renewal, it is unconvincing, for the artificiality of the ending seriously mars the total effect of the work. Warren's readiness to resolve the conflicts of a varied and benighted cast of characters demands a suspension of disbelief greater than most readers are able to summon.

III

Robert Penn Warren's latest novel, *Wilderness* (1961), is "a tale," according to its subtitle, "of the Civil War." Episodic in structure, it departs even more radically in form from the earlier novels than did *The Cave*, varying in the direction of greater simplicity. Gone are the brooding disquisitions on truth and history, for Warren has, as his critics have so long advised, dropped his passages of philosophizing in favor of a direct and uncluttered narrative. Nor is the scene of the novel, as the seasoned reader of Warren might expect, set wholly in the South. *Wilderness* opens in Bavaria, shifts to New York City, and reaches its climax in the front lines of Grant's army during the Battle of the Wilderness.

Thematically, however, the novel returns to a favorite Warren problem—the idealist, bemused by the "compulsion of the dream," who is forced to test his vision of reality against the "gigantic conspiracy" of the world.[7] Since a great war would, by its nature, both magnify and simplify the issues involved, Warren has dramatized the dilemma of his idealist by thrusting him into the American Civil War. Finding in the tensions and contradictions of the war an outer manifestation of the inner lives of his characters, Warren has said in his recent long essay, *The Legacy of the Civil War*:[8] "In a civil war . . . all the self-divisions of conflicts within individuals become a series of mirrors in which the plight of the country is reflected, and the self-division of the country a great mirror in which the individual may see imaged his own deep conflicts, not only the conflicts of political loyalties, but those more profoundly personal."

Having treated the idealist heretofore in a mocking or ironic fashion, Warren draws Adam Rosensweig, the hero of *Wilderness*, with obvious warmth and sympathy. Adam, a cripple doomed from birth with a deformed foot, seems destined to live out his life repairing watches in a stagnant Bavarian town where, ironically, time stands still. But determining to go to America to "fight for freedom," he has Old Jacob, the village cobbler, fashion him a special boot braced with straps and buckles which makes him "look almost like anybody else" (17). Jacob, who through adversity has entered into the "awfulness of joy" (31), refuses to take payment for the boot—it is his own investment in the cause of freedom. "You may wear it into battle," he tells Adam, "but it will still be mine" (32). When Adam reveals his plan to his uncle he is dismissed as a fool—a judgment of Adam repeated by every major character in the novel. But there is nothing to hold Adam in Bavaria: his parents are dead, his father's only legacy a love of liberty and an incapacity for serving his own worldly interests. With a satchel containing phylactery, talith, and siddur, the gift of his devout uncle, Adam signs on for America with a boatload of mercenaries.

Adam's idealism is put to the test at once when the recruiter, Duncan, discovers the deformity. Adam insists that his foot would not hinder him in combat, but Duncan, impotent and enraged before such naked idealism, refuses to allow him to debark at New York. At this juncture Adam speculates on the uselessness of his two gifts from Bavaria—the satchel with the objects of devotion and the boot. They came to him in "balanced and mutual inimicalness," for he cannot pray and he will never march for freedom. An anonymous sailor, however, who wishes only to see "if a thing could be done," contrives Adam's escape from the ship. When Adam, thinking to find in his partisan a fellow idealist, tactlessly presses him for his real motive, the sailor blurts out, "ye are a ruddy fool." Ironically, Adam's crippled foot, while heightening his awareness of his difference from other men, makes him curiously insensitive to them.

Once Adam is free in New York, his idealism is further tested by the discovery that not all Yankees are selflessly dedicated to Negro freedom. Rather than wanting to die to make men free, they are demonstrating against conscription by lynching every Negro they can find. Caught up in the riots raging in the city, Adam is saved from death at the hands of the mob by a Negro, Mose Talbutt, who gets him safely to the home of Aaron Blaustein. When Adam tells Blaustein, a friend of his uncle in Bavaria, of his plan to join the army, the older man looks pityingly at the deformed foot, seeing in it the congenital defect all men have at birth. "There is always something from birth," he tells Adam. "There is yourself" (71).

Unable to persuade Adam to stay with him in New York, Blaustein finds Adam a place as assistant to a sutler, Jed Hawksworth, who is leaving for the South. Hawksworth, a North Carolinian who had been driven from the South years earlier for daring to defend a falsely accused slave, despises in Adam the idealism he himself has long since repudiated. The story of Jed's selfless act strikes a responsive chord in Adam, but he finds he cannot admire or even respect his sullen employer. Mose Talbutt, who, it develops, is a runaway slave and deserter, accompanies them as Jed's other assistant. Mose rechristens Adam "Slew" for his deformity, thus initiating Adam's search for identity in the usual fashion of Warren's heroes. Adam pities Mose and tries to help him, but he can feel no warmth for him as an individual.

Adam's experiences on the trip to the lines seem to challenge the worth of his pilgrimage and his father's teaching that there is no nobler fate than to die for human liberty. At a farm where the three men camp, Adam comes upon a German immigrant, a man much like himself, who lies dying of a wound

received at Chancellorsville. As he sits by the man's bedside, sickened by the stench of the suppurating wound, Adam
becomes aware of the apparent futility of the man's actions.
At Gettysburg, only months after the battle, Adam listens to
a drunken harangue on the better part of valor from the
Falstaffian Mordacai Sulgrave. When the three men finally reach
the army in winter quarters, Adam is further discountenanced
by the aimless violence and casual lusts of the liberators. The
Federal soldiers are as cynical, coarse, and prejudice-ridden as
are, apparently, the men of the Confederacy. But Adam continues
to search for some "way to affirm his history and identity in
the torpid, befogged loneliness" of America (163).

The three men, each in his own way an outcast, become
more deeply involved in their reciprocal needs. Jed increasingly
relies on his two assistants, and in his dependence comes to
despise the quiet competence of Adam and the sullen arrogance
of Mose. Jed torments Mose until, goaded beyond endurance,
Mose murders him. Earlier the same night Mose, on his part,
had driven Adam to curse him savagely. Mose flees after the
murder, and Adam, wondering guiltily why he was not the
victim, concludes that "Mose had not been able to kill him
because he had once saved him."

> So Jed, he decided, had had to die in his place. And then, with
> that thought, he wondered if every man is, in the end, a
> sacrifice for every other man. He did not know. He could not
> read the depth of that thought, but stared down into it as into
> a deep well where a little light glimmers on the dark water.
>
> (302)

When the murder of Jed and the consequent flight of Mose
leave Adam suddenly "free" in the Wilderness of Virginia, he
begins to perceive dimly that his desire to fight for freedom
is, like the quest of Amantha Starr, but the inversion of his
need to set himself free. He starts down the trail alone with
the sutler's wagon, but his newly found freedom brings him
only a curious sense of devaluation, "of sad ghostliness." In the
isolation that defines him, he feels his identity draining away.

Stopping in a silent glade where the Battle of the Wilderness rages about him, Adam feels himself in the "cold center of stillness in the storm which was the world" (290).

While musing on the chain of circumstances that brought him from Bavaria to a scrub forest in a hostile land, he is surprised by several tattered and barefoot Confederate soldiers who plunge into the glade, strip him of his boots, and commandeer his supplies. Adam, watching these defenders of slavery ravenously devouring his food, feels a warm gush of pity and blesses them unawares. Abruptly, Union soldiers charge into the glade, and in the melee, Adam seizes a rifle and kills one of the Confederate "scarecrows," a man of "most commonplace face." The eruption of violence, the frenzied and senseless slaughter, subsides as quickly as it began, and Adam is left in the glade with his victim at his feet.

Adam again reflects on the forces which have led him to this point in his odyssey, thinking of all the things which might have been different *if*—"He could not think that *if*. But he had to. He knew that, in the end, he would have to think every *if*— every *if* which was life." (302). Instead of dying for liberty, he is himself stained with the blood of a Confederate soldier. He is suddenly filled with the desolating knowledge that he has been a victim, betrayed by everything and everyone in whom he had believed. And in a sudden excess of anguish he glimpses the black depths of his own motivation: "*I killed him,* he thought, *because his foot was not like mine.*" Hardened by this new knowledge, Adam coldly reaches down to pull the boots off the feet of the dead soldier. They are, he sees, Union boots, so the Confederate must have taken them from a Federal soldier. "*Now it is my turn,*" Adam thinks. Starting to put on the boots, he catches sight of the satchel with its phylactery and talith. Somehow they survived the vicissitudes of his life in America and now lie strewn across the ground. At the sight, Adam's new found sense of power and mastery dies within him. As if to define the terms of his dilemma, Adam stands between boot and satchel, his legacy from Bavaria. He looks again into the face of the dead man. "Am I different from other men?"

he asks himself. And then he finds himself suddenly able to pray: "Have mercy upon the remnant of the flock of Thy hand, and say unto the Destroying Angel, Stay thy hand" (309).

Adam knows that now he will put on the boots, not Old Jacob's boots that make him "look almost like anybody else," but ordinary boots worn by anonymous men of both armies: "He could try, he thought, to be worthy of their namelessness, out of what they, as men and in their error, had endured." He will put on the boots not in vindictiveness and arrogance, but in humility and recognition of the human communion. He is at last reconciled to his own past; he would live it all over again but, as he cries out, "*with a different heart!*"

Such a summary of *Wilderness* oversimplifies Warren's conception by abstracting from their dramatic context the psychological states through which Adam passes. The conclusion of the novel is powerful and persuasive, carrying a greater sense of conviction than the similarly "resolved" endings of *Band of Angels* and *The Cave*. Warren has managed this effect with an economy of means rare in his fiction. The long case histories, the garrulous reminiscences, the diaries and journals of his early novels are eschewed, and with a few strokes he creates characters as sharply realized as a dry-point etching. Warren has always had a tendency to let minor characters seize control of the narrative and, with their own fascinating histories, elbow the star from the center of the stage. But in *Wilderness* the minor characters are rigorously subordinated to the central concern of the hero. Warren has also reduced the war to the scale that matters, the human scale, and he keeps firmly focused on individuals, avoiding the temptation to exploit the more glamorous aspects of the war. General Grant appears only fleetingly, and the great battles—Antietam, Gettysburg, Chancellorsville—are only names in the novel. The only scene of combat is the skirmish which concludes *Wilderness,* a matter of a handful of hungry, lost, and demoralized men chasing one another through the woods.

In Adam Rosensweig, the Old World Innocent adrift in a corrupt New World, Warren has reversed the roles made familiar by so many heroes of Henry James; for, paradoxically, some "fantastic innocence" (206) is necessary for a European to plumb the depths of American corruption. And Warren evidently intends Adam to be representative of a type, described in *The Legacy of the Civil War*, which he believes to be increasingly rare in modern America: "Those men from conflict and division rose to strength. From complication they made the simple cutting edge of action. They were, in the deepest sense, individuals; that is, by moral awareness they had achieved, in varying degrees, identity."⁹

IV

If Robert Penn Warren were to write nothing after *Wilderness*, his place in our literature would still be secure. The quantity of his production is itself impressive. But despite the amount and variety of his work, he has held himself to a consistently high level of craftsmanship. From the beginning of his career, his analytical power and creative force have been disciplined by his critical intelligence and tempered by his formidable erudition. Warren's concern with literature is fundamental and inclusive. His discussions of other writers reveal this deeply serious commitment, for his criticism is warm in its enthusiasm and generous in its judgments, neither excessively formal nor overly intellectual.

Nor are Warren's fiction and poetry rigidly formalistic. In fact, as Eric Bentley once observed,¹⁰ Warren very nearly fulfills our idea of the romantic genius. There is about his art the prodigality of the writer who exercises his verbal gifts for the sheer magic of the effects he can produce. Warren's language is robust and rhetorical. He likes his adjectives and nouns to go in pairs, reinforcing one another, begetting rhythm and resonance. When a comparison catches his fancy, his first metaphor is likely to suggest another, and he piles image on image as he warms to his task. As a result, he is led by his own ingenuity into the excesses of language which mar many otherwise fine passages. About all of Warren's work there is a gusto and masculine force, a willingness to risk bathos and absurdity, reminiscent of the writer who, Warren has said, has had the greatest influence on his own work—Shakespeare.

One of the advantages of surveying all of Warren's writing is the awareness it gives us of his vitality and versatility. Warren's latest poetry, *You, Emperors,* and novel, *Wilderness,* testify to his desire to seek new solutions to artistic problems, and he will undoubtedly continue to grapple with what he has called the "special sickness and dehumanizing distortions of the 1960's."[11] He has always seemed driven to explore the boundaries of his art, to push the possibilities of his form to its outer limits. Warren has said on more than one occasion that writing is a process of exploration, a means of probing and testing in which the artist discovers his meanings and, in defining them, defines himself. In 1957 he told an interviewer for the *Paris Review:* "All writing that is any good is experimental; that is, it's a way of seeing what is possible—what poem, what novel is possible. . . . You put the question to human nature—and especially your own nature—and see what comes out. It is unpredictable."[12] After four decades on the American literary scene, Robert Penn Warren is one of the rarest of all literary figures—a writer who remains unpredictable.

Notes and References

Chapter One

1. Thomas Nelson Page, *The Old South* (New York, 1908), p. 84.
2. *Writers at Work*, ed. Malcolm Cowley (New York, 1959), p. 191.
3. *Thirty-Six Poems* (New York, 1935), p. 28.
4. Michel Mohrt, "Robert Penn Warren and the Myth of the Outlaw," *Yale French Studies*, X (1953), 70; *Segregation: The Inner Conflict in the South* (New York, 1956), pp. 7-8.
5. "Robert Penn Warren," *Wilson Library Bulletin*, XIII (June, 1939), 652.
6. *Ibid.*
7. Randall Stewart, *American Literature and Christian Doctrine* (Baton Rouge, 1958), p. 3.
8. *Writers at Work*, pp. 186-87.
9. *Wilson Library Bulletin*, p. 652.
10. For my discussion of Warren's relationship with the Fugitives, I have relied on Louise Cowan's informative and authoritative *The Fugitive Group: A Literary History* (Baton Rouge, 1959).
11. Cowan, p. 107.
12. Donald Davidson, *Southern Writers in the Modern World* (Athens, Georgia, 1958), p. 16.
13. Cowan, p. 107.
14. *Fugitives' Reunion: Conversations at Vanderbilt*, ed. Rob Roy Purdy (Nashville, 1959), pp. 116-17.
15. *Writers at Work*, p. 192.
16. Allen Tate, "*The Fugitive* 1922-1925: A Personal Recollection Twenty Years After," *The Princeton University Library Chronicle*, III (April, 1942), 81-82.
17. Cowan, p. 150.
18. *Ibid.*
19. Tate, p. 82.
20. *Writers at Work*, p. 192.
21. Davidson, pp. 21-22.
22. Cowan, p. 150.
23. Sidney Hirsch, one of the founders of the Fugitive group.
24. *Fugitives' Reunion*, p. 119.
25. Cowan, pp. 216-17.
26. *Ibid.*, p. 247; John L. Stewart, "Robert Penn Warren and the Knot of History," *ELH*, XXVI (March, 1959), 103.
27. *Fugitives' Reunion*, p. 209.
28. *Ibid.*, p. 99.
29. *Writers at Work*, p. 194.
30. *Ibid.*, p. 191.
31. Twelve Southerners, *I'll Take My Stand*, introduction by Louis D. Rubin, Jr. (New York, 1962), p. 59.

32. *Ibid.*, p. xix.

33. *Writers at Work*, p. 194.

34. *Ibid.*

35. *Fugitives' Reunion*, p. 210.

36. *Wilson Library Bulletin*, p. 652.

37. Harvey Breit, *The Writer Observed* (New York, 1956), pp. 132-33. Interview of June 25, 1950.

38. *An Anthology of Stories from the Southern Review*, eds. Cleanth Brooks and Robert Penn Warren (Baton Rouge, 1953), pp. xi-xvi.

39. Ray B. West, Jr., *The Short Story in America, 1900-1950* (Chicago, 1952), p. 77.

40. *Stories from the Southern Review*, p. xiii.

41. *Selected Essays* (New York, 1958), p. xi.

Chapter Two

1. Robert Lowell, "John Ransom's Conversation," *Sewanee Review,* LVI (Summer, 1948), 388.

2. Warren had earlier written in praise of Ransom in "John Crowe Ransom: A Study in Irony," *Virginia Quarterly Review,* XI (January, 1935), 93-112.

3. John Crowe Ransom, "The Teaching of Poetry," *Kenyon Review,* I (Winter, 1939), 82.

4. Louise Cowan, *The Fugitive Group: A Literary History* (Baton Rouge, 1959), pp. 216-17.

5. "The Themes of Robert Frost," *Selected Essays* (New York, 1958), p. 125.

6. This pattern is described in some detail in John L. Stewart, "The Achievement of Robert Penn Warren," *South Atlantic Quarterly,* XLVII (October, 1948), 562-79.

7. Among the early appreciations of Warren's poetry, I have particularly profited from Cleanth Brooks, *Modern Poetry and the Tradition* (Chapel Hill, 1939), pp. 77-87.

8. John M. Bradbury, *The Fugitives: A Critical Account* (Chapel Hill, 1958), p. 183.

9. "Robert Penn Warren Reads from His Own Works," *Yale Series of Recorded Poets,* Carillon Records, New Haven, Connecticut.

10. "A Note on Three Southern Poets," *Poetry: A Magazine of Verse,* XL (May, 1932), 110.

11. *Modern Poetry: American and British,* eds. Kimon Friar and John Malcolm Brinnin (New York, 1951), pp. 542-43.

12. *Ibid.*

13. "The Themes of Robert Frost," p. 120.

Chapter Three

1. *Writers at Work*, ed. Malcolm Cowley (New York, 1959), p. 191.

2. These stories were collected in *The Circus in the Attic* (New York, 1948).

Notes and References

3. *Writers at Work*, p. 188; John L. Stewart, "Robert Penn Warren and the Knot of History," *ELH*, XXVI (March, 1959), 106; Leonard Casper, *Robert Penn Warren: The Dark and Bloody Ground* (Seattle, 1960), p. 100.

4. J. Létargez, "Robert Penn Warren's Views of History," *Revue des Langues Vivantes*, XXII (1956), 533-43. See also, John G. Miller, *The Black Patch War* (Chapel Hill, 1936) and J. O. Nall, *The Tobacco Night Riders* (Louisville, 1939).

5. *Selected Essays* (New York, 1958), pp. 178-79.

6. *Writers at Work*, p. 188.

7. Malcolm Cowley, "Luke Lee's Empire," *New Republic*, CIX (August 23, 1943), 258.

8. "Introduction," *All the King's Men* (New York, 1953), p. iii.

9. *Writers at Work*, p. 190.

10. *Selected Essays*, p. 81.

11. Willard Thorp, *American Writing in the Twentieth Century* (Cambridge, Mass., 1960), p. 119.

12. "William Faulkner," *Selected Essays*, pp. 59-79.

13. "T. S. Stribling: A Paragraph in the History of Critical Realism," *American Review*, II (February, 1934), 463-64.

14. "An American Tragedy," *Yale Review*, LII (Autumn, 1962), 3.

15. "Introduction," *All the King's Men*, p. iv.

16. Edmund Wilson, *Axel's Castle* (New York, 1931), p. 25.

Chapter Four

1. *Fugitives' Reunion*, ed. Rob Roy Purdy (Nashville, 1959), p. 208.

2. "Introduction," *All the King's Men* (New York, 1953), pp. i-ii.

3. *Ibid.*, p. iii.

4. Harvey Breit, *The Writer Observed* (New York, 1956), p. 132.

5. Hodding Carter, *The Aspirin Age* (New York, 1949), p. 339.

6. George E. Sokolsky, "Huey Long," *Atlantic Monthly*, CLVI (November, 1935), 526.

7. Hartnett T. Kane, *Louisiana Hayride* (New York, 1941), p. 225.

8. "Introduction," *Stories from the Southern Review*, eds. Cleanth Brooks and Robert Penn Warren (Baton Rouge, 1953), xiii.

9. Louis D. Rubin, Jr., "All the King's Meanings," *Georgia Review*, VIII (Winter, 1954), 422.

10. "Introduction," *All the King's Men*, p. v.

11. *Ibid.*, p. vi.

12. *Ibid.*, p. iv.

13. John Edward Hardy, "Robert Penn Warren's Double Hero," *Virginia Quarterly Review*, XXXVI (Autumn, 1960), 583-97.

14. "Introduction," *All the King's Men*, p. vi.

15. Norton R. Girault, "The Narrator's Mind as Symbol: an Analysis of *All the King's Men*," *Accent*, VII (Summer, 1947), 220-43.

16. "Introduction," *All the King's Men*, p. ii.

17. See "Love and Separateness in Eudora Welty," *Selected Essays* (New York, 1958), pp. 156-69.

18. Francis Fergusson, "Three Novels," *Perspectives U.S.A.*, VI (Winter, 1954), 33.

19. See William M. Schutte, "The Dramatic Versions of the Willie Stark Story," *All the King's Men: A Symposium* (Pittsburgh, 1957), pp. 75-90; Leonard Casper, *Robert Penn Warren: The Dark and Bloody Ground* (Seattle, 1960), pp. 116-21, 133-36.

20. Wolcott Gibbs, *The New Yorker*, January 24, 1948, p. 45.

21. *Selected Essays*, p. 57.

22. Frederick A. Pottle, "Modern Criticism of *The Ancient Mariner*," *Essays on the Teaching of English*, eds. E. J. Gordon and E. S. Noyes (New York, 1960), p. 261.

23. Richard Harter Fogle, "The Romantic Movement," *Contemporary Literary Scholarship* (New York, 1958), p. 126. Warren's essay continues to excite critical controversy. See J. B. Beer, *Coleridge the Visionary* (London, 1959); E. B. Gose, Jr., "Coleridge and the Luminous Gloom," *PMLA*, LXXV (June, 1960), 238-44; Humphrey House, *Coleridge* (London, 1953); Elisabeth Schneider, *Coleridge, Opium, and Kubla Khan* (Chicago, 1953).

24. *Selected Essays*, p. 222.

25. *Ibid.*, p. 228.

26. "Writer at Work: How a Story Was Born and How, Bit by Bit, It Grew," New York *Times Book Review*, March 1, 1959, p. 5.

27. See above, pp. 75-76.

28. "Writer at Work," p. 5.

Chapter Five

1. *Selected Essays* (New York, 1959), p. 48.

2. *Writers at Work*, ed. Malcolm Cowley (New York, 1959), p. 196.

3. James H. Justus, "Warren's *World Enough and Time* and Beauchamp's *Confession*," *American Literature*, XXXIII (January, 1962), 500-11.

4. *Selected Essays*, p. 55.

5. "About the Author," *Saturday Review of Literature*, XXXIII (June 24, 1950), 11.

6. *Selected Essays*, p. 39.

7. *Ibid.*, p. 54.

8. "The Way It Was Written," New York *Times Book Review*, August 23, 1953, p. 6.

9. *Ibid.*

10. *Writers at Work*, p. 189.

11. "The Way It Was Written," p. 6.

12. *Ibid.*

13. *The Legacy of the Civil War* (New York, 1961), p. 50.

14. *Writers at Work*, p. 188.

15. Leonard Casper, *Robert Penn Warren: The Dark and Bloody Ground* (Seattle, 1960), p. 188.

16. Leslie A. Fiedler, "Romance in the Operatic Manner," *New Republic*, CXXXIII (September 26, 1955), 29.

Notes and References

17. John M. Bradbury, *The Fugitives: A Critical Account* (Chapel Hill, 1958), p. 228.

18. Delmore Schwartz, "The Dragon of Guilt," *New Republic*, CXXXIX (September 14, 1953), 17.

Chapter Six

1. *Writers at Work*, ed. Malcolm Cowley (New York, 1959), p. 195.

2. *Selected Essays* (New York, 1958), p. 186.

3. "Writer at Work: How a Story Was Born and How, Bit by Bit, It Grew," New York *Times Book Review*, March 1, 1959, p. 5.

4. *Poet's Choice*, eds. Paul Engle and Joseph Langland (New York, 1962), p. 80.

5. Cleanth Brooks, *The Hidden God* (New Haven, 1963), p. 117.

6. Frederick Lewis Allen, *Only Yesterday* (New York, 1931), pp. 193-94.

7. For an excellent analysis of *Wilderness* to which my own discussion is indebted see Cleanth Brooks, *The Hidden God*, pp. 120-25.

8. *The Legacy of the Civil War* (New York, 1961), pp. 83-84.

9. *Ibid.*, p. 90.

10. Eric Bentley, "The Meaning of Robert Penn Warren's Novels," *Forms of Modern Fiction* (Bloomington, Indiana, 1948), p. 271.

11. "Elizabeth Madox Roberts: Life Is from Within," *Saturday Review*, XLVI (March 2, 1963), 38.

12. *Writers at Work*, p. 198.

Selected Bibliography

PRIMARY SOURCES

A. *Books*

John Brown: The Making of a Martyr. New York: Payson and Clarke, 1929.
Thirty-Six Poems. New York: Alcestis Press, 1935.
Night Rider. Boston: Houghton Mifflin Co., 1939. (Reissued by Random
  House, 1948.)
Eleven Poems on the Same Theme. Norfolk, Connecticut: New Directions,
  1942.
At Heaven's Gate. New York: Harcourt, Brace and Co., 1943. (Reissued
  by Random House, 1959).
Selected Poems, 1923-1943. New York: Harcourt, Brace and Co., 1944.
All the King's Men. New York: Harcourt, Brace and Co., 1946. (Modern
  Library edition with introduction by the author, 1953.)
The Circus in the Attic and Other Stories. New York: Harcourt, Brace
  and Co., 1948.
World Enough and Time: A Romantic Novel. New York: Random House,
  1950.
Brother to Dragons: A Tale in Verse and Voices. New York: Random
  House, 1953.
Band of Angels. New York: Random House, 1955.
Segregation: The Inner Conflict in the South. New York: Random House,
  1956.
Promises: Poems 1954-1956. New York: Random House, 1957.
Selected Essays. New York: Random House, 1958.
Remember the Alamo! New York: Random House, 1958. Landmark Book
  for children.
The Cave. New York: Random House, 1959.
The Gods of Mount Olympus. New York: Random House, 1959. Legacy
  Book for children.
All the King's Men: A Play. New York: Random House, 1960.
You, Emperors, and Others: Poems 1957-1960. New York: Random House,
  1960.
The Legacy of the Civil War: Meditations on the Centennial. New York:
  Random House, 1961.
Wilderness: A Tale of the Civil War. New York: Random House, 1961.

B. *Textbooks*

An Approach to Literature, eds. Cleanth Brooks, Robert Penn Warren, and
  John T. Purser. Baton Rouge: Louisiana State University Press, 1936.
  Third edition, New York: Appleton-Century-Crofts, Inc., 1952.
Understanding Poetry, eds. Cleanth Brooks and Robert Penn Warren.

New York: Henry Holt and Co., 1938. Third edition, New York: Holt, Rinehart, and Winston, 1960.

Understanding Fiction, eds. Cleanth Brooks and Robert Penn Warren. New York: Appleton-Century-Crofts, Inc., 1943. Third edition, 1960.

Modern Rhetoric, eds. Cleanth Brooks and Robert Penn Warren. New York: Harcourt, Brace and Co., 1949. Second edition, 1958.

C. *Articles in Periodicals*

"A Note on Three Southern Poets," *Poetry, XL* (May, 1932), 103-13.

"The Blind Poet: Sidney Lanier," *American Review,* II (November 1933), 27-45.

"T. S. Stribling: A Paragraph in the History of Critical Realism," *American Review,* II (February, 1934), 463-86.

"John Crowe Ransom: A Study in Irony," *Virginia Quarterly Review,* XI (January, 1935), 93-112.

"Some Recent Novels," *Southern Review,* I (Winter, 1936), 624-49.

"Some Don'ts for Literary Regionalists," *American Review,* VIII (December, 1936), 142-50.

"The Present State of Poetry In the United States," *Kenyon Review,* I (Fall, 1939), 384-98.

"The Way It [*Brother to Dragons*] Was Written," New York *Times Book Review,* August 23, 1953, pp. 6, 25.

"Knowledge and the Image of Man," *Sewanee Review,* LXII (Winter, 1955), 182-92.

"A Lesson Read in American Books," New York *Times Book Review,* December 11, 1955, pp. 1, 33.

"Writer at Work: How a Story Was Born and How, Bit by Bit, It Grew," ["Blackberry Winter"], New York *Times Book Review,* March 1, 1959, pp. 4-5, 36.

"An American Tragedy," *Yale Review,* LII (Autumn, 1962), 1-15.

"Elizabeth Madox Roberts: Life Is from Within," *Saturday Review,* XLVI (March 2, 1963), 20-21, 38.

SECONDARY SOURCES

This is a highly selective list of studies in English about Warren. For a more complete list see Leonard Casper, *Robert Penn Warren: The Dark and Bloody Ground* (Seattle, 1960), pp. 191-208. The Spring, 1960 (Volume VI), issue of *Modern Fiction Studies* is devoted to Warren and includes a checklist of criticism. See also the bibliographical supplement to the *Literary History of the United States,* pp. 234-36.

ANDERSON, CHARLES R. "Violence and Order in the Novels of Robert Penn Warren," *Hopkins Review,* VI (Winter, 1953), 88-105. Thoughtful analysis of Warren's first four novels in terms of the movement from violence to order.

BENTLEY, ERIC. "The Meaning of Robert Penn Warren's Novels," *Kenyon Review,* X (Summer, 1948), 407–24. Penetrating discussion of the theme of self-knowledge in Warren's first three novels.

BRADBURY, JOHN M. *The Fugitives: A Critical Account.* Chapel Hill: University of North Carolina Press, 1958. Excellent chapters on Warren's poetry and fiction through 1956.

BROOKS, CLEANTH. *The Hidden God: Studies in Hemingway, Faulkner, Yeats, Eliot, and Warren.* New Haven: Yale University Press, 1963. Best short account of Warren's characteristic themes with special attention to the Christian elements in his writing.

——. *Modern Poetry and the Tradition.* Chapel Hill: University of North Carolina Press, 1939. The pages devoted to Warren's poetry are the best early account of his work.

CASPER, LEONARD. *Robert Penn Warren: The Dark and Bloody Ground.* Seattle: University of Washington Press, 1960. The first book-length study of Warren. Many useful critical insights but rather loosely organized. Excellent bibliography.

COWAN, LOUISE. *The Fugitive Group: A Literary History.* Baton Rouge: Louisiana State University Press, 1959. Indispensable for its account of Warren's relations with the Fugitives.

COWLEY, MALCOLM, editor. *Writers at Work: The Paris Review Interviews.* New York: The Viking Press, 1959. A primary source of information for Warren's personal life and his attitude toward his writing.

DAVIDSON, DONALD. *Southern Writers in the Modern World.* Athens: University of Georgia Press, 1958. Useful for its reminiscences of Warren as a student at Vanderbilt and his connection with the Fugitives.

GIRAULT, NORTON R. "The Narrator's Mind as Symbol: An analysis of *All the King's Men,*" *Accent,* VII (Summer, 1947), 220-34. Penetrating analysis of the symbolism of rebirth and the handling of point of view.

LÉTARGEZ, J. "Robert Penn Warren's View of History," *Revue des langues vivantes,* XXII (1956), 533-43. Valuable for its account of the historical background of *Night Rider.*

McDOWELL, FREDERICK P. W. "Psychology and Theme in *Brother to Dragons,*" *PMLA,* LXX (September, 1955), 565-86. An ambitious but too condensed, and consequently obscure, explication.

RUBIN, LOUIS D., JR. "All the King's Meanings," *Georgia Review,* VIII (Winter, 1954), 422-34. Excellent critical account of *All the King's Men.*

SOCHATOFF, A. FRED, editor. *All the King's Men: A Symposium.* Pittsburgh: Carnegie Press, 1957. Seven essays of varying merit on various topics.

STEWART, JOHN T. "The Achievement of Robert Penn Warren," *South Atlantic Quarterly,* XLVII (October, 1948), 562-79. Argues persuasively that Warren's work centers around a single theme—man's efforts to flee from the problem of evil and his ultimate return to that problem.

——. "Robert Penn Warren and the Knot of History," *ELH,* XXVI (March, 1959), 102-36. Contains many insights into Warren's work but is marred by its rather arbitrary categorizing of his heroes.

TATE, ALLEN. "*The Fugitive,* 1922-1925," *Princeton University Library Chronicle,* III (April, 1942), 75-84. An informal and witty reminiscence of the Fugitive years.

Index

Index